NEW HAMPSHIRE

AND THE

Revolutionary War

Bruce D. Heald, PhD

THE
History
PRESS

Published by The History Press
Charleston, SC 29403
www.historypress.net

First published 2013

ISBN 9781540208668

Library of Congress CIP data applied for.

Notice: The information in this book is true and complete to the best of our knowledge. It is offered without guarantee on the part of the author or The History Press. The author and The History Press disclaim all liability in connection with the use of this book.

CONTENTS

Introduction   5

Chapter 1: The French and Indian War   7
Chapter 2: A Period of Revolution in New Hampshire   19
Chapter 3: The American Revolutionary War   53
Chapter 4: New Hampshire Regiments and Militias   73
Chapter 5: Distinguished Patriots of the Revolutionary War   83
Chapter 6: The Major Forts in the War   107

Appendix: The Declaration of Independence of the
   United States of America   117
Bibliography   121
Index   125
About the Author   128

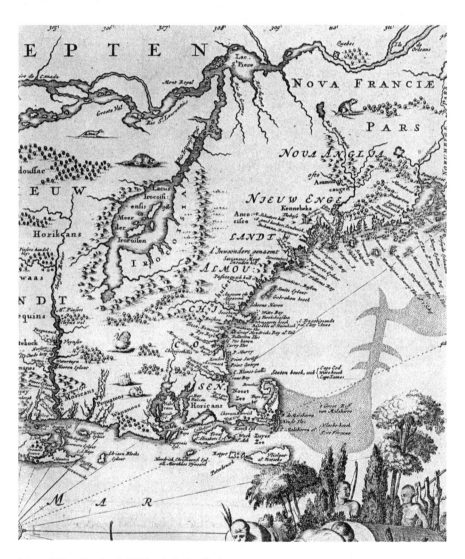

Map of New England, 1600s. *Author's collection.*

INTRODUCTION

To know the American people, we must understand the infinite drive and determination of a people to succeed, a freedom of adventure, the challenge of abandoning the old for the new, the lure of an ever-receding frontier and the restless movement in search of fulfilled life—a search for identity, individualism, freedom, a journey of moral struggle and the struggle of rebellion versus conformity.

Here was created an increasingly free and competitive political system. The growth of self-rule emerged in the colonies from customs and control of Britain. Certain places and people in the history of the world have suddenly emerged from local places into national significance.

The mounting dictates of a faraway ministry had convinced the American colonists that the only alternative to risking death was to live under a form of despotism alien to Americans since they first arrived on this continent.

The Boston Port Bill of 1774, initial punishment for the Boston Tea Party, had turned out to be only a starter. It was the flood of punitive parliamentary acts that came swiftly after the Boston Port Bill that tipped the scale for war—acts that sought to stamp out hard-won charter rights. Even the British administration called these "coercive measures." Typically, thirty-six members of the Governor's Council would be picked in London and appointed by writs, for no longer would they be elected by the people's House of Representatives. Judges and juries would be strictly directed by London. Most detested of all was the act euphemistically called "An act for better regulating the government of the provinces."

The British never suspected that the war with France (the Seven Years' War, called in part the French and Indian War) would be a training ground for future battles in a revolution against the Crown. However, many Patriots in the colonies earned some very important experiences politically and militarily, for during the French and Indian War, they gained experience for a new republic.

Although New Hampshire contributed more men than any other state, no battles were fought within its borders. Some men enlisted for a one-hundred-acre bounty, but most Loyalists laughed at the "rabble in arms." British general William Howe noted that the most able men had joined the army of George Washington, not King George III.

New Hampshire Patriots joined the ranks in the Revolution in order to defend and preserve the freedom and liberty for which they believed.

This text will include information and stories about the involvement and legacy of New Hampshire militias, regiments, rangers, heroes and men of distinctions. Also discussed are the causes and effects of the war, the military campaigns for both the French and Indian War and the Revolutionary War and the major battles in which New Hampshire played an important part in bringing about a new world order.

Chapter 1

THE FRENCH AND INDIAN WAR

T he Treaty of Aix-la-Chapelle, which concluded in 1748, provided for the restoration to each combatant party of all that had been acquired by conquest in the War of Austrian Succession. According to Hobart Pillsbury's *New Hampshire: A History*:

> *A plan of union and organization of the colonies was agreed upon, and submitted to the home government and to the Legislature of each colony. It was not acceptable to the Crown because under it the colonies assumed too much power, and they, in turn, disapproved of it because the powers were too meager. It consequently developed upon each colony to act without a formal political union, and according to the directions from the English authorities.*

New Hampshire contributed several regiments for distant operations and maintained a large number of garrisons for the defense of the less remote frontiers.

Under the command of Colonel Joseph Blanchard, the First Regiment raised five hundred troops and joined the other troops at Crown Point, New York, in 1755. That same year, the Second Regiment sent three hundred troops under the command of Colonel Peter Gilman.

In 1756, a third regiment was raised and placed under the command of Colonel Nathaniel Meserve. The Earl of Loudon was so impressed with its performance that he authorized the organization of a permanent corps of New Hampshire. There were three companies, under the commands of Robert Rogers, John Stark and William Stark. They became famous as Rogers' Rangers. The destruction of the Indian village of St. Francis was one of their most noteworthy accomplishments. Another regiment was contributed by this province, and Nathaniel Meserve was also elected commander of it. Part of the regiment was sent to General Webb at Albany until Lieutenant Colonel Goffe and the remainder under Colonel George Meserve joined the army under the Earl of Loudon at Halifax. Lieutenant Colonel Goffe's command was part of the force employed in the defense of the Fort William Henry against the body of French and Indians under the command of Louis-Joseph de Montcalm. At the end of an engagement of six days, the fort surrendered due to the lack of supplies and ammunition. The French had agreed that the garrison should go out with dignity and honors of war and should be escorted by them to Fort Edwards with the baggage.

As the New Hampshire troops were marching near the rear, they were attacked by the Indians, and out of two hundred men, eighty were killed. The French withdrew to Canada. General Webb called on the colonies for additional troops. New Hampshire responded by raising 250 troops, who were placed under the command of Major Thomas Tash. General Webb stationed the command at Fort at Number 4, Charlestown. From this moment onward, the British and colonial armies progressed successfully during further engagements.

Garrison fort on the upper shore of the Connecticut River. *Author's collection.*

In 1758, New Hampshire sent another regiment of eight hundred troops, under Colonel John Hart, that participated in the operations under General James Abercrombie.

In 1759, the successes of both the British and colonial forces were most decisive. Ticonderoga was taken under the command of General William Johnson. The memorable skirmish at the Plains of Abraham between the British under General James Wolfe and the French under the command of Montcalm occurred later that year. There in Quebec, these two great commanders laid down their lives in battle.

In the autumn of that same year, Major Rogers and his corps of rangers destroyed the Indian town of St. Francis. After twelve days, the men were obliged to leave their duties, and many of them perished in the attempt to regain the New Hampshire settlement. (The engagement of Benjamin Bellows and his troops at Keene and that of John Kilburn at his home in Walpole during 1755 are among the most famous encounters.)

There is an interesting statement that appeared in a report of a committee charged with raising a regiment for the operations at Crown Point, as recorded by Hobart Pillsbury in *New Hampshire*:

> *The men of this province, having long been inured to war, can be expected to render better service in the field, while other colonies which have had less experience in this direction, could more advantageously be subjected to demands for money and material. Mr. Parkman, in his summary of what had been done for the mother country, and for themselves by the colonies in the last French and Indian war, observed that, notwithstanding the paucity of her resources, "New Hampshire had put one in three of her able-bodied men into the field."*

MILITIA BATTLES IN THE SEVEN YEARS' WAR

During these early colonial years, the state militia served in all the colonial battles, as well as the expeditions that captured the Fortress of Louisbourg in 1745 and Port Royal, Nova Scotia, in 1710. During the French and Indian War, the New Hampshire militia supplied about five thousand men for the major campaigns, including men who served in Rogers' Rangers. These provincial soldiers gallantly served at the following battles during the French and Indian War.

Fort at Number 4, Charlestown, New Hampshire. *Author's collection.*

The Battle of Lake George, 1755

The Battle of Lake George was conducted in the north of the province of New York on September 8, 1755. The battle was a campaign by the British to eliminate the French from North America. The French forces amounted to 1,500 French, Canadian and Indian troops commanded by Jean Erdman, Baron de Dieskau. The 1,500 colonial troops were commanded by William Johnson and 200 Mohawks led by Chief Hendrick Theyanoguin.

According to Fred Anderson in his *Crucible of War*:

> *William Johnson, who had recently been named the British agent to the Iroquois, arrived at the southern end of Lac Saint Sacrement on 28 August 1755 and renamed it Lake George in honor of his sovereign George II. His intention was to advance via lakes George and Champlain to attack French-held Fort St. Frederic at Crown Point, which was a keystone in the defense of Canada.*

Baron de Dieskau had left Crown Point to set up an encampment at Fort Carillon, which was situated between the two lakes. On September 4, Dieskau decided to launch a raid on Johnson's base camp at Fort Edwards on the Hudson River. Historian Fred Anderson noted, "His plan was to destroy the boats, supplies and artillery that Johnson needed for his campaign."

In his *History of the United States*, historian George Bancroft wrote, "Leaving half his force at Carillon, he led the rest of that alternate route to the Hudson, landing his men on an alternate South Bay and marching them along Wood Creek." Dieskau arrived on September 7, 1655, near Fort Edwards with his troops of French regular grenadiers, Canadian militia, Abenakis and Caughnawaga Mohawk allies.

Baron de Dieskau ordered his Canadians and Indian troops to attack Johnson's camp. Fred Anderson noted that the Caughnawagas "did not wish to attack an entrenched camp, the defenders of which included hundreds of their Mohawk kinsmen. The Abenakis would not go forward without the Caughnawagas and neither would the Canadians." Dieskau assembled his French troops and led them along the Lake Road to where Johnson's camp was located. Once Dieskau's troops were located in the open field, the American gunners loaded with grapeshot and cut "lanes, streets and alleys" through the French troops. When Johnson was wounded, he was forced to retire to his tent. When Dieskau went down with serious wounds, the French retreated and abandoned the attack.

It was Colonel Joseph Blanchard, commander of Fort Edwards, who saw the smoke from this encounter and promptly sent Nathaniel Folsom's company of eighty men of the New Hampshire Provincial Regiment and forty men from the New York Provincial Regiment under the command of Captain McGennis to investigate the situation, as reported by C.E. Porter in his *History of Manchester*:

> *Hearing the report of guns in the direction of the Lake, they pressed forward, and when within about two miles of it, fell in with the baggage of the French army protected by a guard, which they immediately attacked and dispersed. About four o'clock in the afternoon, some 300 of the French army appeared in sight. They had rallied, and retreated in tolerable order. Captain Folsom posted his men among the trees, and as the enemy approached, they poured in upon them a well-directed and galling fire. He continued the attack in this manner till prevented by darkness, killing many of the enemy, taking some of them prisoners, and finally driving them with many of the enemy's packs he brought in, thus securing the entire baggage and ammunition of the French army. In this brilliant affair, Folsom lost only six men, but McGennis was mortally wounded, and died soon after. The loss of the French was very considerable.*

W. Max Reid's *The Story of Old Fort Johnson* provided the conclusion of the battle, recording that the French troops who were killed in this engagement were mostly Canadians and Indians but not the French regulars, who were thrown into the pool "which bears to this day the name of Bloody Pond. The English loss killed, wounded and missing at the battle of Lake George was 262, and that of the French, by their own account, was 228."

Fred Anderson concluded that "all though the battle itself was inclusive, the strategic result at Lake George was significant, Johnson was able to advance a considerable distance down the lake and consolidated his gain by building Fort William Henry at its southern end." Anderson also wrote that had Dieskau succeeded in halting Johnson at Fort Edwards, it would have not only ended the threat to Fort St. Frederic but would also have "rolled back New York's and New England's defenses to Albany itself."

The Siege of Fort William Henry, 1757

The Siege of Fort William Henry was conducted during the month of August in 1757 by the French general Louis-Joseph de Montcalm against the British-held Fort William Henry. The fort was located at the southern end of Lake George, between the British province of New York and the French province of Canada. Stationed there were a force of British regular troops and provincial militia under the command of Lieutenant Colonel George Monro. After several days of battle, Monro finally surrendered to Montcalm, whose force included about two thousand Indians. The surrender included the withdrawal of the garrison to Fort Edwards. The terms also included the note that the French military would protect the British from the Indians as they withdrew from the fort.

According to Ian K. Steele's *Fort William Henry & the Massacre*:

> *Montcalm's Indian allies violated the agreed terms of surrender and attacked the British column, which had been deprived of ammunition, as it left the fort. They killed and scalped a significant number of soldiers, took as captives women, children, servants, and slaves and slaughtered sick and wounded prisoners. Early accounts of the events called it a massacre, and implied that as many as 1,500 people were killed even though it is unlikely more than 200 people were actually killed in the massacre.*
>
> *The exact role of Montcalm and other French leaders in encouraging or defending against the action of their allies, and the total number of*

casualties incurred as a result of their actions, is a subject of historical debate. The memory of the killing influenced the actions of British military leaders, especially those of British General Jeffery Amherst, for the remainder of the war.

The French and Indian War began in 1754 over real estate disputes between the North American colonies of France and Great Britain in western Pennsylvania and New York. The first years of the conflict proceeded poorly for the British.

Fort William Henry was a rough square fortification that was designed to repel any Indian attacks, but it was not prepared to withstand any enemy that had artillery. The fort was only capable of housing four to five hundred troops.

During the winter of 1756–57, the fort was garrisoned by several hundred men from the Forty-fourth Provincial Regiment Militia commanded by Major Will Eyre.

According to historian William R. Nester:

> *In March 1757 the French sent an army of 1,500 to attack the fort under the command of the Governor's brother, Pierre de Rigaud. Composed primarily of colonial troupes de la marine, militia, and Indians, and without heavy weapons, they besieged the fort for four days, destroying outbuildings and a large number of watercraft before retreating. Eyre and his men were replaced by Lieutenant Colonel George Monro and the 35th Foot established his headquarters in the entrenched camp where most of his men were located.*
>
> *Intelligence was communicated from Fort Edward in April that the French were accumulating resourced and troops for an attack on Fort William Henry. On July 23, a detachment of Connecticut rangers commanded by Major Israel Putnam were sent onto the lake for reconnaissance. They returned with word that Indians were encamped on islands just 18 miles from the fort. On the August 2, Lieutenant-Colonel John Young with 200 regulars and 800 Massachusetts Militia were sent to reinforce the garrison at William Henry. The reinforcement increased the size of troops to approximately 2,500; some in poor health.*

As noted in the first volume of Francis Parkman's *Montcalm and Wolfe*:

> *While Montcalm's Indian allies had already begun to move south, his advance force of French troops departed from Carillon on 30 July under*

Levis' command, travelling overland along Lake George's western shore because the expedition did not have enough boats to carry the entire force. Montcalm and the remaining forces said they left the next day, and met with Levis for the night at Ganaouske Bay. The next night, Levis camped just three miles from Fort William Henry, with Montcalm far behind.

Early on the morning of August 3, Levis and the Canadians blocked the road between Edward and William Henry, skirmishing with the recently arrived Massachusetts militia. Montcalm summoned Monro to surrender at 11:00 am. Monro refused, and sent messengers south to Fort Edward, indicating the dire nature of the situation and requesting reinforcements. Webb, feeling threatened by Levis, refused to send any of his estimated 1,600 men north, since they were all that stood between the French and Albany. He wrote to Monro on August 4 that he should negotiate the best terms possible; this communication was intercepted and delivered to Montcalm.

Montcalm, in the meantime, ordered Boulamaque to begin siege operations. The French opened trenches to the northwest of the fort with the objective of bringing their artillery to bear against the fort's northwest bastion. On August 5, French guns began firing on the fort from 2,000 yards, a spectacle the large Indian contingent relished. The next day a second battery opened fire from 900 feet further along the same trench, creating a crossfire. The effect of the garrison's return fire was limited to driving French guards from the trenches, and some of the fort's guns were either dismounted or burst due to the stress of use. On August 7, Montcalm sent Bougainville to the fort under a truce flag to deliver the intercepted dispatch. By then the fort's walls had been breached, many of its guns were useless, and the garrison had taken significant casualties. After another day of bombardment by the French, during which their trenches approached another 250 yards, Monro raised the white flag to open negotiations.

Historian William Nester noted that "[t]he terms of the surrender were that the British, and their camp followers, would be allowed to withdraw under French escort, to Fort Edwards, with the full honours of war, on condition that they refrain from fighting for 18 months. They were allowed to keep their muskets and a single symbolic cannon, but no ammunition."

The following morning, before the British began to form for the march to Fort Edwards, the Indians renewed attacks on the defenseless British. At 5:00 a.m., Indians entered huts in the fort that were housing the wounded British, who were supposed to be under the care of French doctors, and killed and scalped them. Immediately, Monro complained that the terms of capitulation had been violated, but his contingent was forced to surrender some of its baggage in order to even be able to begin the march. As the British left, they were surrounded and harassed by swarming Indians, who grabbed their weapons and clothing, including that of the female and young slaves and servants.

According to Revolutionary War historian William P. Nester, "On the 14th of August, Montcalm wrote letters to Loudoun and Web, apologizing for the behavior of the Indians, but also attempting to justify it."

Historian Ian Steele wrote that

> [O]n September 27 a small British fleet left Quebec, carrying paroled or exchanged prisoners taken in a variety of actions including those at Fort William Henry and Oswego. When the first fleet arrived at Halifax, about 300 people captures at Fort William Henry were returned to the colonies. The fleet continued on to Europe, where a few more former captives were released; some of these also eventually returned to the colonies.

The events of the battle and subsequent killings were depicted in the 1826 novel *The Last of the Mohicans* by James F. Cooper, as well as in the film adapted from the book.

Historians disagree as to the assigned responsibility for the Indian action. Francis Jennings contended that Montcalm anticipated what was going to happen and deliberately ignored it when it did happen.

The Battle of Carillon (Ticonderoga), 1758

This battle was fought on July 8, 1758, near Fort Carillon (presently known as Fort Ticonderoga) on the shore of Lake Champlain between the British colony of New York and the French colony of Canada.

The battle took place primarily on the rise about one mile from the fort, with the French army of about four thousand troops under the command of General Louis-Joseph de Montcalm and General Chevalier de Lévis defeating the superior force of British troops under General James Abercrombie, which assaulted an entrenched French position without using field artillery. The battle was considered the bloodiest of the war, with more than three thousand casualties in all.

American historian Lawrence Henry Gipson wrote of Abercrombie's campaign that "no military campaign was ever launched on American soil that involved a greater number of errors of judgment on the part of those in position of responsibility." Many military historians had cited the Battle of Carillon as a classic example of tactical military incompetence.

Abercrombie was confident of a quick victory and ignored several viable military options, such as flanking the French breastworks, waiting for his artillery or laying siege to the fort. He decided to make a direct assault on the entrenched French without the benefit of artillery.

Montcalm conducted the defense with spirit, but he also committed strategic errors in preparing the area's defenders that a competent attack could have exploited, and he made tactical errors that made the attacker's job easy.

The fort, abandoned by its garrison, was captured by the British the following year, and it has been known as Fort Ticonderoga ever since. Despite several large-scale military movements through the area, during both the French and Indian War and the American Revolutionary War, this was the only major battle fought near the fort's location.

According to historian Rupert Fureaux's *The Battle of Saratoga*:

> *While the fort itself was never endangered by the British assault, Ticonderoga became a byword for impregnability. Even though the fort was effectively handed to the British by a retreating French army in 1759, future defenders of the fort and their superior officers, who may not have been familiar with the site's shortcomings, fell under the spell of this idea. In 1777, when General John Burgoyne advanced down Lake Champlain at the beginning of the Saratoga campaign, General George Washington, who had never seen the fort, thought highly of its defensive value. Anthony Wayne, who was at Fort Ticonderoga preparing its defenses before Burgoyne's arrival, wrote to Washington that the fort "can never be carried without much loss of blood." Fort Ticonderoga was surrendered by the Americans without much of a fight in July 1777.*

The Battle of the Plains of Abraham, Quebec, Canada, 1759

The Battle of the Plains of Abraham, also known as the Battle of Quebec, was a pivotal battle in the Seven Years' War. The battle began on September 13, 1759, between the British army and navy and the French army on the plateau just outside the walls of Quebec City, on land that was originally owned by a farmer named Abraham Martin.

The battle involved fewer than ten thousand troops for both sides but proved to be a deciding moment in the conflict between France and Britain over the eventual fate of New France and later influenced the creation of Canada.

The battle lasted a total of fifteen minutes. British general James Wolfe successfully resisted the column advance of French troops and the Canadian military under Louis-Joseph de Montcalm, using tactics that proved effective against the standard military formations. During the battle, General Wolfe received a blow that ended his life, and Montcalm died the next morning after receiving a musket ball wound just below his ribs.

In the wake of the battle, France's remaining forces in Canada came under pressure from British forces. Within four years, most of France's possessions in eastern North America would be ceded to Great Britain. The Treaty of Paris was signed in 1763 to end the war, and it gave possession of part of New France to Great Britain, including Canada and the eastern half of French Louisiana, which was located between the Mississippi River and the Appalachian Mountains.

Chapter 2

A PERIOD OF REVOLUTION IN NEW HAMPSHIRE

When on that field his band the Hessians fought
Briefly he spoke before the fight began:
"Soldiers, those German gentlemen were bought
For four pounds, eight and seven pence, per man,
By England's King: a bargain, it is thought.
Are we worth more? Let's prove it while we can:
For we must beat them, boys, ere set the sun,
Or my wife sleeps a widow!" It was done.

—*John Stark at Bennington*

The American Revolution began in 1775 and, in many ways, has defined who these Patriots were and what they stood for. Americans made their commitment to build a republic on the concepts of individual liberty, democracy and a constitutional government.

It was time to consider a separation from the mother country. Although the causes of the American Revolution were controversial and complex, a common ideology brought together those wishing to separate from England. That ideology contended that human beings are capable of governing themselves. Many American colonists had become convinced that they were a unique and even superior people. Unfortunately, the new English king, George III, who came into power in 1760, was determined to be a strong ruler and discipline the American colonies firmly under the British government's control.

The American colonies were growing explosively in population and rapidly expanding economically, and they wished to press westward into a new frontier.

AN AMERICAN REVOLUTIONARY WAR COMMITMENT

We were approaching difficult times. The troubles that would lead to the American Revolution had begun. Measured oppression on the part of England was being followed by resistance and violence in the colonies.

In 1759, Great Britain formed the plan of raising revenue from the colonies. The first evidence of this intention was seen in the following year. An order was received by the customhouse officers in America to apply to the Supreme Court for what were called "writs of assistance." These writs were to authorize the persons holding them to enter any ship, store or houses, upon mere suspicion, and search for goods that had been imported in violation of the English acts of trade.

The king kept among the colonies a standing army in times of peace, abolished the free system of English laws in neighboring provinces, took away the Americans' charters and altered the fundamental forms of government.

The king's power was very oppressive for those living in the colonies. The customhouse officers, however, applied to the court for the writs, and the court appointed a time when the propriety of granting them should be discussed. Mr. James Otis, one of the earliest Patriots in the New England colonies, held the position of advocate general, and he was consequently called on to render his legal services in support of the king's officers. (James Otis studied law at Harvard College and practiced his profession for two years in Plymouth, Massachusetts, before moving to Boston.)

Thinking that the writs were tyrannical and oppressive, he refused and resigned his office as advocate general for the British. Being immediately approached by the merchants on the colonial side, he undertook their cause. He was very intelligent and wished to join in the colonial cause, which deeply excited interest in all classes of people in the colonies. The trial took place in the council chambers of the old townhouse.

Government officers were anxious to know whether they would receive the writs that would give them so much power and perhaps enrich them with great wealth. Citizens and merchants were equally desirous to learn if their houses were to be considered inviolable or if they would be opened up to the curiosity of any officer of the customs who chose to disturb them with his suspicions.

Of the speeches pronounced on this occasion by James Otis, the highest praise came from President John Adams. He said that Otis was aflame with fire and a rapid torrent of eloquence. "American independence," Adams continued, "was then to be born. Every man, of an immense crowded audience, appeared to me to go away as I did, ready to take arms against writs of assistance."

The court adjourned for consideration, and although the officers of the court came to no conclusion on the matter, nothing more was heard or said about the writs. From this moment, parties began to form either of friends of the king or friends of the

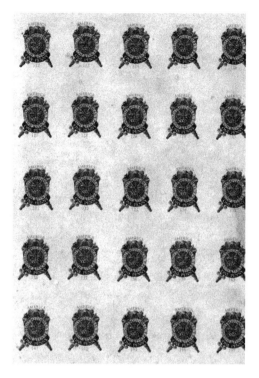

Stamps from the Stamp Act, Revolutionary War Battle Box. *Richard T. Nowitz Collection, Simon & Schuster Children's Publishing Division.*

colonies. The people of Boston and the province of New Hampshire, however, entertained little affection for their friends of the mother country.

In 1765, King George III gave his consent to the famous Stamp Act. This tax was laid on every piece of vellum, parchment or paper on which anything of use to any person could be written or printed. This tax varied from half a penny to twenty shillings.

This stamp was to have been put on every possible document: newspapers, almanacs, cards, marriage certificates, writs of court, customhouse papers—all were to bear a stamp and pay for it. When popular feeling was at its height on this matter in the colonies, news was received in Boston that a cargo of these papers might be daily expected in the harbor. It was also rumored that a gentleman by the name of Andrew Oliver, secretary of the province, had been appointed a distributor of the stamps.

It was at this time that the "Liberty Tree" first came to be noticed. This tree formerly stood at the head of Essex Street in the town of Boston. On

Liberty Tree, etching. *Henry R. Blaney and the Grundmann Studios.*

the morning of August 14, some effigies were found hung, one of which was intended to ridicule Mr. Oliver. The other was a boot with a grotesque figure peeping out of it, having the Stamp Act in its hand, intended to represent Lord Bute, who had done much in Parliament to promote American taxation.

Little business was done that day. People gathered about the streets, talking of the Stamp Act, the British officers and the Liberty Tree. Large numbers came in from surrounding towns to learn what was going on and to join in the expression of popular feeling. The mob gradually increased and became more formidable. A little after twilight, the people formed a procession from the Liberty Tree to the townhouse, where they knew that the governor and his council were holding a meeting. In this place, a building had just been erected by order of Mr. Oliver that they supposed was intended for a stamp office.

The crowd of people immediately leveled it to the ground and carried off the remains in celebration on their shoulders. They proceeded to Fort Hill, where Mr. Oliver resided, and made a bonfire in front of his house. They proceeded to break the windows and tear down the garden fences and, at length, obtained complete possession of his house. It was near midnight when the mob began to grow less noisy; an attempt was made by the government officers to disperse them. These gentlemen, however, were unsuccessful and received rather harsh treatment from some of the townspeople. At midnight, all was over and it became quiet.

Many other affairs of this nature gave sufficient pretense to the military forces in New England to station a detachment of regular troops in strategic stations in New England, specifically in Boston.

Boston Massacre, 1770

"To arms, to arms!" In February 1770, the feeling of the time was demonstrated. The merchants of Boston had agreed not to import British goods. Some, however, were so reluctant of public opinion and interest that they were determined to pursue their trade as usual. They, of course, fell under the censure of their fellow citizens and were objects of contempt.

The papers of March 5 recorded an event of dispute and quarrels between the British soldiers and a mob of people in Boston. This day was to be marked by an event more horrid than any that had yet occurred: the Boston Massacre. This event originated in a slight affray between three or four young men and a soldier who was stationed as sentinel by a little alley that led to the barracks of the Fourteenth Regiment (British).

The main guard of the troops was stationed opposite the townhouse, and they were all marched daily to this place. A mob had been collected by the resistance and was ready for an attack, even on the armed soldiers. They shouted for the main guard and soon found the way to the neighborhood of their station. One party found a single sentinel standing before the door of the customhouse, which was a building now occupied as a bank on State Street.

This event occurred on a clear moonlit evening, and there was some snow on the ground. As the mob approached, the sentinel went to the door of the small house and knocked three or four times to apprise those within of the danger. Word was soon sent to the lieutenant of the main guard of the expected assault, and he dispatched a company of six troops, to the relief of the sentinel. Captain Thomas Preston, commander of the regiment, immediately followed them.

The mob of local people formed in a semicircle about the steps of the customhouse. Mr. Henry Knox, a bookseller and later a famous general of the Revolution, went from the guardhouse with Captain Preston, having his hand on his shoulder while walking to the scene, and warned him of the consequences of firing on the mob. By this time, all the bells were ringing,

Above: *The Boston Massacre*, State Street in 1770, drawn for Ballou's Pictorial Drawing-Room Company, 1855, Boston, Massachusetts. Artist unknown.

Left: Testimony of a witness to the Boston Massacre, taken on the following day. *Mellen Chamberlain Autograph Collection.*

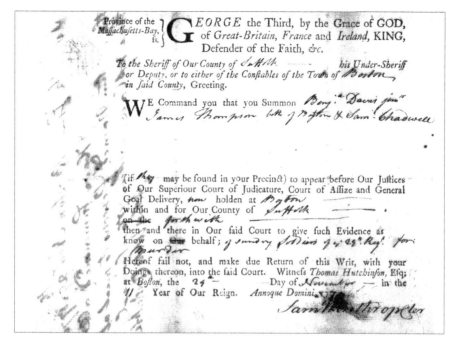

Summons for the appearance of witnesses in a separate trial of Captain Preston's men. *Mellen Chamberlain Autograph Collection.*

and people had collected from every direction to ascertain what was going on. They pressed and crowded upon the soldiers, and some attacked them with pieces of ice or snow and clubs, while from all sides were shouts of, "Fire, fire, if you dare."

At length, the soldiers commenced firing, and three of the citizens were killed on the spot. Two others were mortally wounded, and several were considerably injured. A cry was soon raised through the town of, "To arms, to arms, turn out with your guns," and the drums were beating and the bells ringing. The king's council immediately assembled, and the people were assured that Captain Preston and his men would be delivered to the magistrates.

The funeral of the slain was attended with great ceremony and by an immense multitude; shops were closed, and all the bells of Boston were tolled along with those of the neighboring town and other towns from across the province of New Hampshire. The procession formed on King Street and marched through the town to the burial ground, where the bodies were placed.

In the course of a few days, all the troops were moved to the "Castle Island" in Boston Harbor. Captain Thomas Preston was tried and

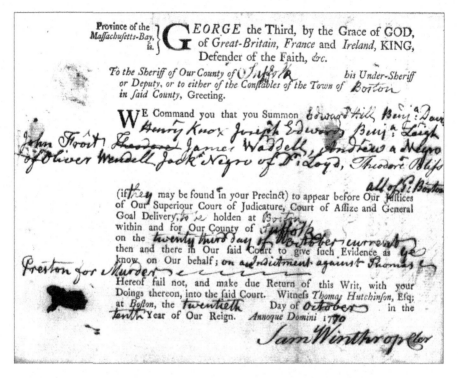

Summons for the appearance of witnesses in the trial of Captain Preston. *Mellen Chamberlain Autograph Collection.*

acquitted. The soldiers were tried soon after. They were defended by John Adams and Josiah Quincy Jr. Two were convicted of manslaughter, and the other six were acquitted. These acquittals were highly creditable to the citizens of the town. Even in the midst of a deep excitement and great indignation, it was evident that they were governed only by the strictest sense of duty and justice.

When the news of the Boston Massacre reached New Hampshire, the citizens of Exeter held a town meeting and voted in favor of domestic manufacturers of tea, and of the non-consumption of British tea. Governor John Wentworth tried to satisfy the people of that town by appointing Peter Gilman to the Governor's Council.

According to historian Hobart Pillsbury's *New Hampshire:*

> *In October 1771, the ship "Resolution" docked at Portsmouth with a hundred hogsheads of molasses on board. About midnight on October 29 "a numerous company" of men in disguise and armed with clubs went*

aboard the vessel and seized the molasses. Governor Wentworth offered a reward of $200 for evidence leading to the conviction of these rioters, but the names of the "numerous company" was never divulged an the smuggling of the cargo of the "Resolution" was never punished.

Later, on that same day that the Boston tea party was taking place, the citizens of Portsmouth held a mass meeting, at which they advocated a union of all the colonies, and it was decided that in cast the East India Company imported any tea at Portsmouth, the inhabitants would prevent its being landed or sold. On June 25, 1774, the ship "Grosvenor" docked at Portsmouth with 27

New Hampshire governor John Wentworth, from a painting by John S. Copley. *From Hobart Pillsbury's* New Hampshire: A History.

chests of tea and the tea was carted to the Custom-house. A mass meeting of citizens was held, at which the Governor attended on horseback. A committee of 11 was appointed to take up the matter with the consignee of the tea, and by agreement the merchants shipped the tea to Halifax, so that there was no Portsmouth tea party.

In the House of Representatives on May 28, 1774, notwithstanding Governor Wentworth's protest of illegality, it was "voted that the Honorable John Wentworth, Speaker of the House, Samuel Cutts, John Giddings, Clement Marsh, Josiah Bartlett, Henry Prescott and John Pickering be a Committee of this House to correspond as occasion may require with the Committees that are or may be appointed by the several Houses of Representatives in our sister Colonies, and to exhibit to this house an account of such of their proceedings when required."

The First Overt Act Against England, 1774–1781

The first armed resistance in New Hampshire against Great Britain occurred on December 14, 1774, when a party of Patriots under the command of Captain Thomas Pickering of Portsmouth attacked Fort William and Mary at New Castle, took it and confined its captain, John Cochran, and its garrison of five men. They broke open a magazine, took from it one hundred barrels of powder and sixty stand of arms and claimed from the ramparts sixteen pieces of cannon. This may be called the opening ball of the Revolution. Its importance may be appreciated from the fact that Major John Demeritt of Durham hauled an ox cart load of this powder to Cambridge, and it was then dealt out to our troops there prior to the Battle of Bunker Hill.

The powder was also distributed to the upriver towns. Some was carried to Exeter, Newmarket and Durham. It was first stored under the pulpit of the meetinghouse at Durham, but thinking it unsafe there, Major Demeritt of Madbury had a magazine built for it, leading from his cellar, where it was stored until wanted for use.

The attack was made on Fort William and Mary for the purpose of securing the military stores. Paul Revere rode directly from Boston to inform the Patriots that a detachment of royal troops had been ordered to the Piscataqua to secure the fort. The Patriots were none too early in their expedition, for a day after, two British ships of war arrived in the harbor with a detachment of troops from Boston, took possession of the fort and dismantled it.

During the summer of 1774, troops continually arrived in the port towns and worked to construct fortifications and barracks. Early in September, two hundred of the British soldiers sailed up the Mystic River and stole from the powder house a large quantity of powder that belonged to the province.

The state of affairs became very serious in New England and the major ports therein. Every effort was made to arm the people and provide them with such provisions as they would need in time of war. In carrying these from town to town in the country, the inhabitants were obliged to be very cautious in order to deceive the guards posted throughout the countryside. Cannonballs were concealed in loads of manure and powder and shot in the baskets of the merchants, as well as in candle boxes.

A NEW REVOLUTIONARY GOVERNMENT: THE END OF THE PROVINCE

Judge Leslie P. Snow, in his tercentenary address at Portsmouth in 1923, described the situation when Governor Wentworth decamped in 1775:

> With the exile of the royal governor, the imperial government, which had ruled for ninety years ceased to function. The province, then containing over one hundred towns, averaging over eight hundred inhabitants each, was left without any supreme authority. Commissions existing under the authority of the Crown were annulled. Courts were closed and magistrates were shorn of their power.
>
> Here came to the surface of intelligence, initiative and individualism of the people which from the days of the early "combination" had so many times been in evidence. The local government of the towns supplemented by the good examples of influential citizens and the good sense of the people sufficed to maintain public order. The Exeter convention assumed control over inter-colonial and military affairs, and gradually extended their direction over domestic and civil matters. They provided for post offices and issued paper currency.
>
> For the most part, however, their power was exercised through a provincial committee of correspondence, which came to be known as a committee of safety, sometimes acting through its satellites, the committees in the towns. The instruction of the people to this committee have been likened by our early historian, Dr. Belknap, who saw them in their execution, to those given by the Romans to their dictators, to take under consideration all matters in which the welfare of the province in the security of their rights is concerned and to take the utmost care that the public sustain no damage.

A TIME OF REVOLT: LEXINGTON AND CONCORD IN 1775 AND THE "SHORT HEARD 'ROUND THE WORLD"

In March 1775, public sentiment was disturbed and quite excited by the disgraceful conduct of the British troops. On April 14, 1775, General Thomas Gage received secret orders from the Earl of Dartmouth to proceed against the open rebellion that existed in the colony, even at the risk of a conflict. On April 18, General Gage dispatched a body of about eight hundred troops to destroy the military stores that had been collected at Concord, a town about eighteen miles from Boston. However, loyal Patriots got wind of the plan and sent Paul Revere and William Dawes by separate routes on their famous rides to spread the alarm in Lexington to Concord. It was from the belfry that a lantern signal was given indicating, "One by land, and two if by sea, and on the opposite shore will be." A tablet was placed on its front on October 17, 1878, with the inscription:

The signal lanterns of Paul Revere
Displayed in the steeple of this church, April 18, 1775,
Warned the country of the march of
The British troops to Lexington and Concord.

CHRIST CHURCH, SALEM STREET.

Christ Church, Salem Street (Old North Church). *Author's collection.*

Having reached Lexington on April 19, 1775, six miles distant from Concord, the British were met by a company of militia that had been hastily assembled from the different towns upon the first alarm. It was about sunrise. The British troops advanced at a quick march to within a few rods. Under command of Lieutenant Colonel Francis Smith, they called out in a loud voice, "Disperse, you rebels, thrown down your arms and disperse."

The company of militia was too small to risk a confrontation. While the men dispersed, the British shouted and, by a discharge from their ranks, killed several in the company. Shortly thereafter, they resumed their march to Concord, where they destroyed a few articles of stores and sixteen barrels of flour. The Americans had already carried off most of their stores, but the

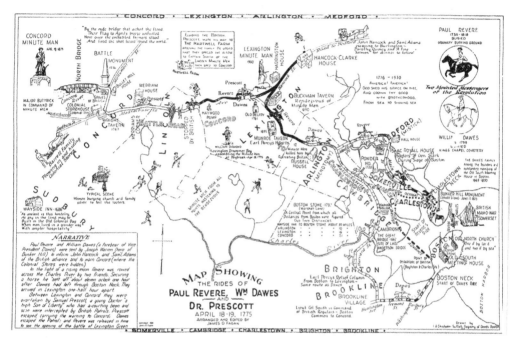

Map showing the rides of Paul Revere, William Dawes and Dr. Preston, April 19, 1775. Arranged and edited by James O. Fagan. *A. Chisholm, etcher, Suffolk Registry of Deeds, Boston.*

Battle of Lexington by J. Rogers. *Author's collection.*

British and American battle on the *Concord Bridge*, by A. Lassell Ripley. *Union Provident Corporation.*

British destroyed what they could (guns, carriages, entrenching tools, flour and a liberty pole).

At Concord's North Bridge, the growing American forces inflicted 14 casualties on a British platoon, and at about noon, Lieutenant Colonel Smith began marching his troops back to Boston. The militia by then had collected a considerable number of men. Being enraged at the loss of the companions, they made a bold and furious attack on the enemy and drove them back to Lexington. Hearing of the situation of his troops, General Gage sent a sizable reinforcement, with two fieldpieces, to assist the troops. The united forces amounted to about 1,800 men.

At Lexington, a relief column under Brigadier General Hugh Percy lessened the pressure of militia attacks. In their retreat, the regular troops were pursued with great strength and vigor from neighboring militias. From the cover of trees and stone walls, the undisciplined farmers were able to thin the ranks of the enemy with much success. During the day, the situation of the British forces was extremely hazardous. Worn down with fatigue and exhaustion, they reached Charlestown at about seven o'clock in the evening, with the loss of 273 men, killed, wounded and taken prisoners. The next day, they arrived in Boston.

Hostilities had now commenced in earnest. The strongest excitement prevailed throughout all of the New England colonies. The country militias

The Battle of Lexington, engraved by James Smillie. *Alonzo Chappell.*

assembled from every quarter in Middlesex County in great numbers, and in the course of two days, Boston reached a complete state of blockade. Liberty poles were erected in almost every village, and all who fell under suspicion were obliged to make a public display of the loyalty.

The following day, General Hugh Percy reported the following:

> *In obedience to your Excellency's orders, I marched yesterday morning at 9 o'clock with the 1st Brigade and the 2nd field pieces, in order to cover the retreat of the grenadiers and light infantry in their return from their expedition to Concord. As all the houses were shut up, and there was no appearance of a single inhabitant, I could get no intelligence concerning them till I had passed Menotomy, when I was informed that the rebels had attacked his Majesty's troops, who were retiring, overpowered by numbers, greatly exhausted and fatigued, and having expanded almost all their ammunition—and at about 2 o'clock I met then retiring from the town of Lexington—I immediately ordered the 2 field pieces to fire at the rebels, and drew up the brigade on a height.*
>
> *The shot from the cannon had the desired effect, and stopped the rebels for a little time, who immediately dispersed, and endeavored to surround us being*

very numerous. As it began now to grow pretty late and we had 15 miles to retire, and only 36 rounds, I ordered the grenadiers and light infantry to move at first; and cover them with my brigade sending out very strong flanking parties which was absolutely necessary, as there was not a stone wall, or house, though before in appearance evacuated, from whence the rebels did not fire upon us. As soon as they saw us begin to retire, they pressed very much upon our rear guard, which for that reason, every now and then, I believe…

In this manner we retired for 15 miles under incessant fire all around us, till we arrived at Charlestown, between 7 and 8 in the evening, and having expanded almost all our ammunition. We had the misfortune of losing a good many men in the retreat, though nothing like the number which from many circumstances I have reason to believe were killed of the rebels. His Majesty's troops during the whole of the affair, behaved with their usual intrepidity and spirit nor were they a little exasperated at the cruelty and barbarity of the rebels, who scalped and cut off their ears of some of the wounded men who fell into their hands.

Respectfully,
General Hugh Percy

The Battle of Lexington aroused the people of New Hampshire to the sense of great danger. At the Fourth Provincial Congress, Colonel Nathaniel Folsom of Exeter was selected to be brigadier general of a command of New Hampshire troops. At a subsequent convention at Exeter on May 17, 1775, steps were taken to arm for the Revolution. Two thousand troops were authorized. General Folsom was appointed major general, with three regiments under his command. The regiments were commanded by Colonel James Reid, Colonel Enoch Poor and Colonel John Stark.

Toward the end of May, the British army was reinforced with considerable numbers. About the middle of June, General Gage issued a proclamation in which he declared the province of Massachusetts, of which New Hampshire was a part, to be in a state of rebellion, and he offered pardon to all those who would resort to his standard. He was pleased, however, to deny pardon to John Hancock and Samuel Adams.

According to Hobart Pillsbury, the officers of the army of 1775 were as follows:

One of the majors in Colonel Stark's First New Hampshire Regiment in 1775 was Andrew McClary of Epsom. He fought at Bunker Hill and was killed by a stray shot from a British ship in the river.

A captain under Stark was Isaac Baldwin, of Hillsborough, who was the sixth settler of that town in 1766. He fought with Stark in the Seven Years' War in 20 battles. He was killed at Bunker Hill.

Joseph Cilley, of Nottingham, was major in Colonel Poor's Second Regiment. He was one of the patriots engaged in the attack on Fort William and Mary in 1774 and marched at the head of 100 men to the battle of Lexington. He later became colonel of Stark's regiment and after the war was major-general of the militia.

Colonel James Reid, of the Third Regiment, came from Fitzwilliam. He became blind after the hardships of camp life and retired from the army in 1776 and is buried in Fitchburg, Massachusetts.

The surgeon of his regiment was Dr. Ezra Green, of Dover, who later became surgeon on board the "Ranger" under command of John Paul Jones. He was a member of the constitutional convention and lived to be 101 years old until he died at Dover in 1847.

Aftermath: Casualties: *American: 50 killed and 39 wounded*
                              British: 73 killed and 174 wounded

A RESPONSE OF THE MINUTEMEN

Many momentous events were to follow in rapid succession. New Hampshire's response to the challenge of Lexington was magnetic. Just as it had been first to attack, it was now the first to answer the call of a sister colony when assailed. After all, Boston was and is considered the "Cradle of Liberty."

According to Hobart Pillsbury:

Upon receipt of news of the first bloodshed of the Revolution, the beacons were lighted upon New Hampshire hilltops and our men sprang to arms. John Stark left his work at his mill and hastened to the scene of conflict. While traveling he called his men and ordered them to assemble in Medford.

Within four days more than 2,000 men, representing nearly every territorial unit of the province, had reported to him for duty, among who were many veterans who had served under him during the battle at Ticonderoga. The leading and decisive part, which John Stark and his men took in the battle of Bunker Hill, [came] two months later.

The New Hampshire volunteers fought independently with the other provincial forces, using the powder captured from Fort William and Mary. The effective marksmanship of Stark's men, their coolness under fire, and their gallantry in covering the retreat of the other colonists turned a rout into a virtual victory, the moral effect of which was of vital importance.

At the Fourth Provincial Congress, opening on May 17 the same year, 133 delegates were present. Matthew Thornton was chosen as president and Ebenezer Thompson as secretary. Among the first acts of this Congress, whose sessions were extended over a period of about six months, was the adoption of a resolution—given that the evident purpose of the British government was to "subjugate this and the other American Colonies to the most abject slavery"—to provide "for the raising immediately of 2,000 effective men in the province including officers and those already in the service, their enlistment to continue until the last day of December, unless the Committee of Safety, appointed the same day should judge it proper that a part or the whole be discharged sooner."

NEW HAMPSHIRE IN THE BATTLE OF BUNKER HILL, 1775

The American commanders obtained information that the British intended to post themselves on Bunker Hill. The position was a very important one to the British, and they were determined to take it for their advantage. Accordingly, on June 16, a band of one thousand provincials under the command of Colonel Prescott was sent to take possession of the Bunker Hill station.

At no time and in no place before June 17, 1775, had there been any conflicts that committed the colonists to revolution in order to maintain their rights under the Crown or that determined their capacity to successfully withstand the attacks of disciplined royal troops under the command of generals who had gained renown on European battlefields.

A small army of Patriots, scarcely organized and almost wholly undisciplined, gathered around Boston to prevent the British soldiery whom occupied the town from attempting further incursion to destroy military stores and harness the people in the colonies. The two armies were too close together to remain quiet or postpone bloodshed for too long. The British were restricted on the land side of Boston, and the colonists were not secure in their position either. Inevitably, each army tried to

View of the North End of Boston and of Charlestown, circa 1764. *Author's collection.*

improve its situation and condition. Word reached the patriots that the British intended to seize and fortify Bunker Hill and Dorchester Heights; immediately, the Committee of Safety of the Massachusetts Provincial Congress recommended to the Council of War that the American patriots take possession of Bunker Hill and fortify it. And it was done. The British attempted to dislodge them. The battle was fought, and Bunker Hill became a word of glory.

It is appropriate that a brief sketch of events preceding the battle and the engagement be provided here.

During April 1775, the British forces in Boston numbered about four thousand troops. Reinforcements soon came so that at the time of the Battle of Bunker Hill, they numbered (including those on armed vessels) fully eleven thousand men. They were commanded by General Thomas Gage, an officer of experience and bravery.

The total number of Americans then encamped about Boston may have slightly exceeded that number. There was not a professional soldier among them. They were volunteers, and they brought with them their muskets, which were of different calibers, hence they were not adapted to the use of prepared cartridges. Some of them were not organized in any formal way, but they were generally in companies or regiments. There were no brigades or divisions. They wore no prescribed uniforms—few, if any, of the soldiers had them. There was no recognized flag, and it is not probable that any flag floated over either the redoubt or the rail fence during this battle.

The Committee of Safety held a meeting on June 15 and determined that "[w]hereas it appears of importance to the safety of the colony that possession of the hill called Bunker Hill in Charlestown, be secured kept and defended...therefore, Resolved, unanimously, that it be recommended to the council of war that the above mentioned Bunker Hill be maintain by sufficient force being posted there." It also appointed a committee to communicate its decision to the Council of War and to consult with the general officers over the matters on importance.

A Council of War was held the next day. It is not known who truly composed this council officially nor what persons were present by invitation, but it is reasonable to assume that Generals Samuel Ward, Israel Putnam, Joseph Warren and Seth Pomeroy were there, and if not originally present, it is very likely that Colonel Prescott was soon called in and informed that he had been selected to command the troops to seize and fortify the hill.

There were five hills on the peninsula of Charlestown, being about one mile long with an average width of nearly half a mile. The three larger ones were known as Morton's, Breed's and Bunker Hills. Each of them is associated with the battle. Morton's Hill was 35 feet high and located near the point where the British landed; they formed their line on its side. Breed's Hill was 62 feet high, and Colonel Prescott built the redoubt on it. Bunker Hill, from which the name of the battle was taken, was 110 feet high and located nearest Charlestown Neck, which is an isthmus connecting the peninsula with the mainland. The "Neck" was narrow and so low that at the highest tides, the water flowed over it. As the Americans had no vessels, it was the only way by which their troops could reach the hills or retreat from them.

Those hills, by their height and proximity to Boston, could command the city and render its hostile occupancy impossible if properly fortified. Colonel Prescott was detailed to that work. It is stated that he was to have had 2,000 men, but later it was ascertained that there were entrenching tools for only half that number. They were ordered to report for duty at sunset on that day at Cambridge Common. This force was made up of about 300 men from his own regiment, 250 each from Massachusetts regiments commanded by Colonels James Frye and George Bridges, and about 120 to 200 men from Connecticut commanded by Captain Thomas Knowlton.

When they were ready to march, it was past nine o'clock in the evening. President Langdon of Harvard College, himself an ardent Patriot who had been elected only the year before from the pastorate of the North

Cambridge Common, with George Washington taking command, as seen in the mural by Charles Hoffbauer. *New England Mutual Life Insurance Company.*

Church in Portsmouth, invoked the blessing of God on that small band of citizen soldiers and the cause the troops represented. Then they marched, and at about 11:00 p.m., they crossed the Neck to Bunker Hill. Here the men were first informed of the duty for which they had been detailed. The entrenching tools had preceded them. It is generally supposed that the Committee of Safety and the Council of War intended to have Bunker Hill fortified. Colonel Prescott, however, said that he had been ordered to fortify Breed's Hill and that he should obey his orders. Many historians believe that Breed's Hill was fortified by mistake, but whether that mistake was in the orders or in the interpretation of them is not known.

It was a bright, starlit evening, and the men worked with pick, bar and spade and with an energy born only of experience in labor and the consciousness of a just cause. They were not paid in shillings and pence but rather in the hope for a free land and a government administered by rulers of their own selection. It is small wonder, then, that in the four hours before dawn, they had thrown up an entrenchment that was a surprise to the British and a credit to their skill.

As their newborn fortification was kissed by the rising sun, the guns of the warship *Lively*, anchored in the Charles River, opened fire on them. The booming guns of the *Lively* awoke the British in Boston. When they discovered that the provincials had occupied and fortified the hill that they were to have taken possession of on the next day, they were surprised and very indignant. Possibly their anger was heightened by the feeling that their purposes had been betrayed and that the army they deigned to despise had stolen a march on them. General Gage called a Council of War. It was decided to attack the provincials at once and to land for that purpose on Morton's Point. It is certain, looking at the redoubt from Copp's Hill in Boston, that the practiced eye of the veteran British general saw that it could be easily flanked along the riverbank. He probably concluded that either the provincials would run or they would be captured without much loss on his part. It is stated that General Gage was of the opinion that it would be hazardous to land either from the Charles or the Mystic Rivers in the rear of the redoubt, thus putting his troops between the forces in the redoubt and the main army at Cambridge.

At that time, and for several hours after, the rail fence had not been occupied or strengthened, and the stone wall on the banks of the Mystic was not erected until after the British had landed. The timely arrival of the New Hampshire regiments and the hasty defenses erected by them and the men of Connecticut changed all this.

General Gage ordered some two thousand men for the attack. They marched with ammunition, provisions, blankets and artillery to Long Wharf, where they embarked in barges and moved toward their landing place. Meanwhile, the vessels of war, taking advantage of the tide, moved nearer to the shore, swept the grounds between the redoubt and Morton's Point to dislodge any troops prepared to resist their landing and enfiladed the Neck to prevent reinforcements coming to the aid of the Americans.

It was considerably past noon when the British landed without opposition. They were under the command of General Howe. Having examined the

Passage to Charlestown.

British passage to Charlestown–Bunker Hill. *Robin Carver.*

American defenses, he asked for reinforcements, and while waiting for their arrival, many of his soldiers dined for the last time. During this delay, their cannons were placed in position, and it was discovered that the guns had been supplied principally with ammunition double their caliber. Thus it happened that the field artillery on both sides were nearly useless.

In the American camp, great excitement prevailed. Bells were rung and drums beaten. At Cambridge, there was more confusion than on Breed's Hill, where the men were in the immediate presence of the enemy. At the time they were on the hill, the Connecticut men were at the rail fence, and the two hundred New Hampshire men under Lieutenant Colonel Isaac Wyman were at the breastwork.

Colonel Seth Read (sometimes "Reed") of New Hampshire arrived with his men at about two o'clock in the afternoon and took position at the rail fence. On the bank of the Mystic River was a strip of unprotected shore that the British general intended to occupy by a flank movement that would place

The Battle of Bunker Hill, painted by Alanzo Chappa. *Author's collection.*

part of his veterans in the rear of the fence, which, being at the same time assaulted in front, could no longer be held by the Americans. The same flank movement would, when successful, render the redoubt no longer tenable.

Upon receipt of his final orders, Colonel John Stark hastened to the front from Medford with the remainder of his regiment. As he passed along the side of Bunker Hill, his skilled eye took in the situation with its imminent dangers, and he at once placed his men in the open space along the river that General Gage intended to utilize. As there were no fortifications there, he ordered his men to pile up stones from the fence to the water's edge, which they did as quickly as possible.

Meanwhile, the British reinforcements arrived on the seventeenth, and their troops were formed in three columns: one to attack the redoubt, another the rail fence and the last to attempt a flanking movement along the river, where Colonel Stark had posted his men and erected the stone barricade. The three columns moved to the attack with the steadiness of veterans and the position of a formal parade. They began firing while at a considerable distance from the defenses and, as their aim was high, inflicted only slight damage. The Americans, on the contrary, were ordered to reserve their fire and aim low. They were excellent marksmen and knew that their safety depended on the accuracy of their muskets. They waited until the attacking party was only eight rods distant. A blaze of fire issued from the American lines, staggering the British veterans, killing and wounding many of them. They continued to advance until met by a second discharge, even deadlier than the first, whereupon they broke and fled down the hill. They were soon rallied and led to the assault again, and again they received such a shower of bullets that no troops could stand against it. They ran from the field, many of them to the water's edge where they had landed. Never had there been a braver assault, and never had undisciplined troops made a braver defense.

It was with some difficulty that the British officers rallied their men. But discipline prevailed, and again their lines were formed. They had discovered the unprotected space between the breastwork and the rail fence, and practically abandoning the attempt to force a passage along the river—where Colonel Stark held the key to the situation—they made an assault on the redoubt, breastwork and open space and carried each at the point of the bayonet. Our men had expended their ammunition and had scarcely enough bayonets with which to meet the onslaught. Many of them clubbed with their guns and fought until hope had fled and they were ordered to retreat. The men at the rail fence were not so hard-pressed; they protected the retreat over Bunker Hill and across the Neck. In this service, they lost more men than during their defense. The British followed our troops to the Neck but did not attempt to cross it or dare to risk a battle with the army encampment at Cambridge.

Nominally, the British had gained a victory, but their losses were nearly two and a half times greater than those of the Americans. A few more battles like this one would have ruined the British army and left the Americans disciplined and strengthened in numbers, courage and efficiency. The Americans were surprised that they had withstood the royal veterans so successfully, and though disappointed and defeated, they felt that their cause was not hopeless, that their defeat was only temporary and that victory would come with greater efficiency in the several departments of their army. The actual victory was with the British; the moral effect, however, was with the Americans. At first, though, it was the expression of disaster and defeat. A quarter century later, it would be the synonym of patriotism and glory, boasting the honor of service and the distinction of command.

The adherents of Putnam and Prescott were so persistent, not to say intentionally unfair, that the just claims of New Hampshire have been pushed aside, and even judicious writers of history have failed to award to Stark and Read and their men the service and honor to which they were certainly entitled.

For several years, Massachusetts and New Hampshire were united under one government, and the same royal governor later ruled both. The people of each colony were of the same ancestral stock and had the same associations, customs, principles, laws and religion. In fact, little, if anything (except colonial boundaries) separated them. They were brothers residing on separate homesteads. There had been some differences of opinion about boundary lines, but they had been settled and peace had prevailed.

During those day of slow communication and slower transportation, it was nearly a month before our Provincial Congress attempted to organize our soldiers into companies and regiments, commission the necessary officers and furnish them with supplies and munitions of war.

In the meantime, some of our New Hampshire men joined Massachusetts regiments already organized, and others organized themselves. All reported to General Artimas Ward for orders of service. All the troops from New Hampshire were in the battle. The same cannot be said of either Massachusetts or Connecticut. Second, no word has been written against the conduct or bravery of any New Hampshire officer or man engaged at that battle. It was recorded by an unknown reporter that the little handful of brave men (in the redoubt) would have been effectually cut off but for the unfailing courage of the provincials at the rail fence and the bank of the Mystic. They had repulsed the army twice; they then held them back in check until the main body had left the hill. Not until then did the Connecticut companies under Knowlton and the New Hampshire soldiers under Stark quit the station that they had nobly defended.

General Stark is reported to have said that New Hampshire men were undisciplined and inexperienced. That is undoubtedly true, but they were quite as well disciplined as those who held the redoubt, as attested by numerous writers and by the undisputed facts of engagement. One writer noted that the "courage and conduct of the provincials that opposed the light infantry (the New Hampshire troops) saved their co-patriots who were overpowered and obliged to retreat from the fort, and who must otherwise have been cut off, as the enemy, but for such opposition, would have been instantly upon the back of the redoubt."

In Captain Bradford's *History of the Battle of Bunker Hill*, published in 1825, he noted:

> *The troops at the rail fence were closely engaged with the column of the British, when those at the redoubt were obliged to retreat. They fought with great bravery, and had hitherto prevented the advance of the enemy, whose plan was to force their way and turn this flank of the provincials. Here*

the New Hampshire men, under Col's. Stark and Reed…gave proofs of a firmness and courage which richly entitled them to the glory of a victory.

At the time of the battle, New Hampshire had only two organized regiments. Both of them were in the fight at Bunker Hill and were the only regiments there in their entirety. All of the other commands were composed of details from one or more regiments.

In Henry M. Baker's *New Hampshire in the Battle of Bunker Hill*, the following profile of the event is given:

Col. Stark wrote, under date of May 18, 1775, from Medford to the New Hampshire provincial congress, that he had 584 men exclusive of drummers and fifers, and that "the remainder are hourly expected."

The New Hampshire congress voted June 3, 1775, that "ten companies of 62 men each, of the regiment now at Medford in Province of Massachusetts, be the first or oldest regiment." The First Regiment in New Hampshire for the defense of America.

General Dearborn, in his account of the battle published in the Port Folio, says Stark had 13 companies, and speaks of Col. Reed's as a small regiment. Gen. Folsom, under date of June 23, 1775, in a letter to the committee of safety, says: "Stark's regiment still consists of 13 companies."

Again in pursuance of a general order dated July 3, 1775, a return of the army was made, and New Hampshire reported three regiments with 98 commissioned officers and staff, 160 non-commissioned officers, 1,201 men present fit for duty, 115 sick, present, 20 sick, absent, 49 on furlough, and 279 on command, a total of 1,922, with an average of 640 men to each regiment. As Stark's Regiment then consisted of 13 companies, and undoubtedly with more men to each company than the other regiments, it is probable that his command actually exceed 800.

Once more, the official returns show that Col. Reed's command sustained a total loss in the battle of 33, and that Col. Stark's regiment had 60 men killed or wounded. [If Colonel Seth Read had a total loss of 33 from 437 men actually in the battle, then Stark's effective force, with a loss of 60, ought to have been not less than 797, which is more than 100 men more than what was claimed for him.]

Every computation made from the best data obtainable justifies that Stark's regiment not less than 657 men were actually engaged with the enemy. If to this number we add the 437 already stated to have been in Reed's regiment and at the rail fence, and the 136 New Hampshire men in the Massachusetts regiments, we have a total of 1,230. If from this number we deduct 19 men in the two New Hampshire regiments who were not residents of the state, we have 1,211 as the number of officers and enlisted men from our state who actually participated in the fight which made Bunker hill forever memorable in the annals of freedom.

It is probable that few, if any, over 2,000 Americans were actually in the battle. Of this number Connecticut furnished about 200, Massachusetts about 600, and New Hampshire about 1,200. Some 300 or 400 more Massachusetts men were on the hill, and many of them assisted in erecting the redoubt and breastwork but were not in the battle.

No battle of the Revolution accomplished more for the patriot cause. Without it, Bennington, Saratoga, and Yorktown might not have been possible. That New Hampshire bore so conspicuous and honorable a part at Bunker hill confers renown upon our state, and in itself is a eulogium upon the brave men whom this society especially represents. We sustain just pride in their work, achievements, and glory.

Aftermath: Casualties: *American: 140 killed and 271 wounded*
                            British: 226 killed and 828 wounded

THE FIRST CONTINENTAL CONGRESS

At about the time of the Battle of Bunker Hill in June, the convention of delegates to the First Congress was in session at the capitol in Exeter. The first New Hampshire delegates to the Continental Congress were John Sullivan and Nathaniel Folsom. In January 1775, the second convention elected as delegates to the Second Continental Congress John Sullivan and John Langdon. Matthew Thornton was president of the convention and for a time was considered the chief executive of the state. (Patriot Matthew Thornton appears in connection with the article on the Declaration of Independence, of which he was a signer.)

One of the main objectives of the convention was to organize an army and take over the official archives from the secretary of the province, Theodore Atkinson.

At this time, two forts were built at a narrow channel on the Piscataqua River, which was about one mile below the town of Portsmouth. The fort on the west side of the channel was known as Fort Washington, and the other on the east side of the channel known as Fort Sullivan. A company of forty troops was stationed at these forts under the command of Captain Robert Parker, and the entire fortification was commanded by Captain Titus Salter. In June, a company of rangers commanded by Captain Timothy Bedel was raised for the defense of the frontiers on the Connecticut River.

Military Campaign of 1775

While the work of preparing and placing into effect a state constitution was going on, the military forces were engaged in the invasion of Canada.

Scene of the Boston wharf as the British head for their ships. *Bostonian Society.*

In September 1775, General Richard Montgomery led an army into Canada by way of Lake Champlain; in this army, seventy-seven New Hampshire troops formed a company under the command of Captain Henry Dearborn. Another force, under the command of General Benedict Arnold, marched from Newburyport, Massachusetts, through the forest of Maine and Canada. The New Hampshire company, under commander Captain Samuel Ward, was in General Arnold's expedition. General Montgomery captured Montreal, and the two armies united in an assault on Quebec that was unsuccessful. Montgomery was killed and Arnold wounded.

The main body of New Hampshire troops remained under General George Washington at the siege of Boston through the winter of 1775–76. On St. Patrick's Day, March 17, 1776, the British evacuated Boston, and the New Hampshire regiments were discharged and returned to their homes.

Petition for a New Government, October 18, 1775

At this time, New Hampshire petitioned that the delegates in the Continental Congress be allowed to organize a government of their own as a means of preventing any confusion. It was not until November 3 that Congress granted the state's request. It was, however, recommended by the Fifth Provincial Congress that there be a true representation of the citizens of the state and that the delegates be authorized to "establish such a form of government as in their judgment will best produce the happiness of the people, and most effectively secure peace and good order in the province during the continuance of the present dispute between Great Britain and the Colonies."

Soon after, Major General John Sullivan urged the body to grant the request of the state, to be allowed to set up an independent government. At that time, General Sullivan sent a letter to Meshech Weare, president of New Hampshire, outlining such a form of government as he deemed desirable for the state's people.

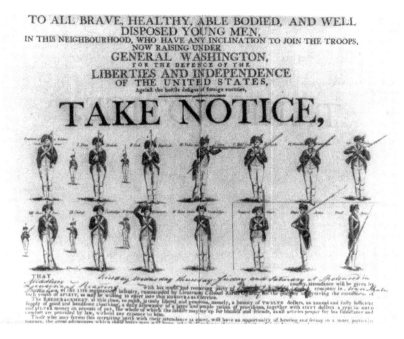

This recruiting poster illustrates the drill for loading the weapon (musket) as a call to arms for the Revolutionary War. Musket drill was an important part to condition the men for battle with the British. *Richard T. Nowitz Collection, Simon & Schuster Children's Publishing Division.*

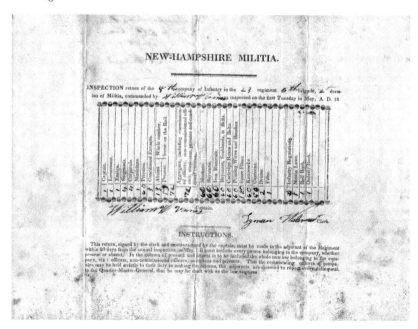

Notice of New Hampshire militia inspection and instructions. *Author's collection.*

Troops Under Arms: A Prelude to War

George Washington. *From Hobart Pillsbury's New Hampshire: A History.*

On December 2, 1775, the Committee of Safety answered the call from General John Sullivan, who was in command at Winter Hill in Charlestown, that men from New Hampshire be sent to Winter Hill in order to replace the troops from Connecticut, who refused to remain there. However, the state had in active duty about 3,000 troops. Accordingly, commissions were sent to men in various towns in order to enlist volunteers for a short term of service so as to replace the Connecticut troops. Thirty-one companies marched to Medford to answer the call. Each company numbered 63 men and was immediately mustered into service by Major Burnham. These New Hampshire troops were called the "Six Weeks Men" and were 2,058 in number; thus, the state had on duty in the field more than 5,000 troops during the month of December 1775.

The First American Constitution to Be Established, 1776

The people of New Hampshire, in conventions with their representatives in town meetings, exercised sovereign powers and developed the principles of the representative.

On December 28, 1775, it was voted in the last convention at Exeter "to take up civil government to continue during the present contest with Great Britain" and thus frame a constitution. It was adopted by the people. This "Constitution of America" provided simple rules for the perpetuation of two houses by annual elections, for their organization and action for appointments of military and civil officers. This constitution became duly effective on January 5, 1776, antedating the federal Declaration of Independence by six months.

Also note that on this date, New Hampshire declared its independence from Britain. It was the first to do so. The Fifth Provincial Congress adopted a temporary constitution. In November, three New Hampshire men—Josiah Bartlett, William Whipple Jr. and Matthew Thornton—signed the Declaration of Independence. They were unable to get to Philadelphia for the July signing due to the lack of funds.

According to Hobart Pillsbury, this first of all written state constitutions is an extremely brief document, containing about nine hundred words, one third of which are devoted to an explanatory preamble.

The first New Hampshire constitution, from in 1776 and presently known in history as a temporary constitution, recorded that

> *the sudden and abrupt departure of His Excellency John Wentworth, our late Governor, and several of the Council, leaving us destitute of legislation, therefore for the preservation of peace and good order, and for the security of the lives and properties of the inhabitants of this colony, we concede ourselves reduced to the necessity of establishing a form of government to continue during the present unhappy and unnatural contest with Great Britain.*

For further information, complete copies of the New Hampshire Constitution are readily available for the public at the statehouse in Concord free of charge.

PORTRAITS OF THE SIGNERS OF THE DECLARATION OF INDEPENDENCE.

The signers of the Declaration of Independence. *From Hobart Pillsbury's* New Hampshire: A History.

Chapter 3

THE AMERICAN
REVOLUTIONARY WAR

It was impossible for colonial citizens then to realize how difficult it would be to revolt against the mother country. In this world of monarchies, the thought of people demanding their rights in order to form their own republican government was an extraordinary adventure. To think that provincials could possibly defeat the most powerful empire in the world for the cause of self-independence seemed to be madness. However, we were a people determined to have freedom from the British monarchy, abandoning the old for the new. According to our declaration to the king of England, it was necessary that our people must:

> *dissolve the political bands which have connected them with another, and to assume among the powers of the earth, the separate and equal station to which the Laws of Nature and of Nature's God entitle them, a decent respect to the opinion of mankind requires that they should declare the causes which impel them to the separation.*

A complete copy of the Declaration of Independence may be found in the appendix.

Military Campaigns of 1776–81

New Hampshire troops participated in the following campaigns in the defense of the Revolution. Military campaigns and operations in January 1776 were, to say the least, failures. For example, in January, the state raised a regiment under the command of Colonel Timothy Bedel for the protection of the frontiers on the Connecticut River. The regiment marched into Canada, and at a fort named The Cedars, the entire regiment surrendered. (Colonel Bedel was not present at the time and could not be held responsible for the regiment's surrender.)

Also, during the same month, a company of field artillery was raised for the defense of Portsmouth, and later in the spring, six additional companies were added. In July, a new regiment was put into the field under the command of Colonel Isaac Wyman, with another under the command of General Joshua Wingate in August. These regiments formed part of General John Sullivan's army in the state of New York. It was assumed that the British, having been driven out of Boston, planed to seize New York and defeat General Washington's army. On August 7, the forces at Portsmouth, under the command of Colonel Pierce Long, were organized into a regiment, and on September 25, the regiment was stationed at New Castle. It later took part in the attack on Fort Ticonderoga in 1777.

The Battle of Trois-Rivieres (Three Rivers), 1776

This battle occurred as part of the American colonists' invasion of Quebec, which had begun in September with the goal of liberating the province from British rule.

The crossing of the St. Lawrence River by the American troops was observed by the Quebec militia, which alerted the British troops at Trois-Rivieres. It was a local farmer who led the Americans into a swamp, enabling the British to land additional troops in the village and establish positions behind the American army. After a brief exchange between the British line and the American troops emerging from the swamp, the Americans broke into a retreat. The British took a sizable number of prisoners, including General Thompson and much of his staff.

This was the final major battle that was fought on Quebec soil. Following defeat, the remainder of the American troops, under the command of John Sullivan, retreated to Fort Saint-Jean and later to Fort Ticonderoga.

Commander in Chief George Washington watches the passing of the Continental army, 1777. *Don Proiani.*

Historian Hobart Pillsbury noted:

> *In September, 1776, New Hampshire raised two more regiments to reinforce Washington's army in New York. One was commanded by Colonel Nahum Baldwin and the other under the command of Colonel Thomas Tash.*

*In December another regiment was raised under command of Colonel David
Gilman. Thus, in 1776, New Hampshire had nine regiments in the field,
which fought under General Washington in Pennsylvania and New Jersey.
Most of the men served six weeks beyond the time of enlistment. They took part
in the battle of Long Island, Washington's retreat across the Delaware.*

In 1777, the British initiated a new movement. General Burgoyne
marched down from Canada with about eight thousand troops and took
Fort Ticonderoga. The purpose of this engagement of the second and third
British armies under the command of General Howe was to unite and cut
off New England from other colonies.

The Battle of Trenton, 1776

The Continental army had suffered many defeats in New York and was
forced to retreat through New Jersey to Pennsylvania. Better than 90 percent
of the Continental army troops who had served at Long Island were gone.
Men had deserted, feeling that the cause for independence was lost. The
morale was very low after so many defeats; a victory in Trenton, however,
would give the men a needed boost.

General Washington moved his troops (fewer than four hundred men) with
him and fell back along the Delaware River, the border with Pennsylvania,
on December 2. General Charles Lee was slowly moving across the state,
General Nathanael Greene had a force covering Washington at Princeton
and other units were scattered around the state.

Two thousand Pennsylvania militia troops joined Washington. He had
all the boats available along the river taken and held with his supplies on
the Pennsylvania side of the river. He repeatedly called for Lee to come to
his support and sent for the New Jersey militia to rally to him. Meanwhile,
the British forces had crossed the state almost unopposed. The New Jersey
militia had showed up with shockingly small numbers of troops. Many of
Washington's troops on hand were under short enlistment due to expire at
the end of the month, desertion was rampant and most all were discouraged.

Lee continued to refuse to come to Washington and was eventually
captured on December 13 in Basking Ridge, New Jersey, by Lieutenant
Colonel Harcourt leading the British dragoons. Under the leadership
of General John Sullivan, the troops then quickly made their way to
Washington's camp. At the same time, General Horatio Gates moved down

from Fort Ticonderoga with eight hundred men to Washington's aid. Both units crossed the Delaware to assemble with General Washington.

The militia showed up in small numbers. Most of the men stayed home to protect their families from the advancing invaders, moving possessions out of the way of the British and Hessians. Joining Washington, the combined armies now moved across the Delaware River to Trenton. Washington had every boat that could be found moved across the river. Now the scene was set for the Battle of Trenton.

Everyone in the American camp felt that the situation was desperate. Colonel Joseph Reed wrote to Washington, saying that "something must be attempted to receive our expiring credit, give our cause some degree of reputation, and prevent a total depreciation of the Continental money, which is coming in very fast—that even a failure cannot be more total than to remain in our present situation." Washington admitted in a letter that "the game was about up." It was recorded on December 22, 1776, that General Washington had about four thousand troops fit for duty.

Washington assembled a staff meeting and decided to attack at Trenton. The Hessians in Trenton were in an exposed position, and it was known that they would be celebrating Christmas on the night of December 25, 1776. Washington decided on a predawn attack on the twenty-sixth, while the Hessian troops and officers were tired—hopefully some were also suffering hangovers. It may have been a misconception that the Hessians were expected to be drunk; some of the officers might have been expected to party late into the night, but not necessarily the troops.

Washington ordered the troops to be ferried across at 5:30 p.m., just after dark, but foul weather and the freezing river slow his progress. Washington's aide, Colonel John Fitzgerald, wrote at 6:00 p.m. as the troops started across, "It is fearfully cold and raw and a snowstorm is setting in. The wind northeast and beats into the faces of the men. It will be a terrible night for those who have no shoes. Some of them have tied only rags about their feet; others are barefoot, but I have not heard a man complain."

Colonel Glover's regiment, from Marblehead, Massachusetts, composed primarily of sailors, manned the boats at McKonkey's Ferry. They managed to get 2,400 troops, horses and eighteen cannons across the icy river. Two other units, one to cross to the south of Trenton at the Trenton Ferry and one farther south at Bristol, were unable to cross or land on the other side due to the bad weather.

Delayed by the weather, Washington's troops did not get across until 4:00 a.m., well behind schedule for a predawn attack. They marched south to Trenton in two columns, one along the river road and the other along the Pennington road, with Generals Sullivan and Greene commanding. Washington commanded the overall operations and rode with General Greene. General Sullivan sent word that his men's muskets would not fire due to being exposed to the storm all night. Washington sent word back in reply on the bayonet: "I am resolved to take Trenton."

At 8:00 a.m., Washington inquired of a man chopping wood if the Hessian sentries were "just outside of Trenton." He pointed to a nearby house, and the Hessians poured out and begin to open fire. The Battle of Trenton had begun.

Moving quickly, both columns moved into Trenton. The Hessians were caught completely unprepared. Colonel Johann Rall, commander of the Hessians, was slow to awaken and dress for battle.

The Hessian officers tried to rally and form their ranks, but the Americans moved too quickly for them. The Americans placed cannons on the rise that controls the two main streets of the town, and the Hessian formations were unable to shape up properly. They tried to get some of their own cannons into action, but these were captured before they could do any damage. The Americans moved aggressively, closing in on the Hessians, breaking up their formations and blocking all the exits to make a front, but some orders were misunderstood, and Hessian regiments became separated.

It is recorded that many Hessians escaped in small groups, but 868 were captured and 106 were killed or wounded. The American army lost perhaps 4 men. They captured several cannons, as well as ammunition and stores. The fighting lasted only ninety minutes. About 600 Hessians, most of whom had been stationed on the south side of the creek, escaped.

Washington had turned the tide from desperately waiting for the axe to fall to aggressive victory, chasing the British forces from the Delaware River and putting them on the defensive, if only for a few days. The battle boosted the confidence of the Continental army and inspired reenlistment of many of General Washington's troops.

In Philip Henry Stanhope's *History of England* (1854), he recorded, "The Hessian soldiers were under the command of Colonel Johann Rall; the Hessians numbered about 1,400 troops. Washington's force comprised 2,400 troops, with infantry divisions commanded by major General Nathanael Greene and John Sullivan, and artillery under the direction of Brigadier General Henry Knox."

The Battle of Princeton

The Battle of Princeton took place on January 3, 1777. On the evening of January 2, General Washington and his Continental army repulsed the British attack at Assunpink Creek in Trenton. That same night, General Washington moved his position, circled around Lieutenant General Charles Cornwallis's army and proceeded to attack the British garrison at Princeton. General Hugh Mercer of the Continental army battled with two regiments of the British army. Mercer's troops were overtaken. Hearing this, General Washington sent some militia commanded by General John Cadwalader to assist General Mercer's fleeing men.

At Princeton, Brigadier General John Sullivan forced the British troops who had taken refuge in Nassau Hall to surrender, thus ending the battle. After this, General Washington moved his army to Morristown the following day, arriving on January 6 at 5:00 p.m. With the victory at Princeton, the

The winter camp at Valley Forge and Morristown. *Granger Collection, New York.*

morale of the American troops rose, and more troops began to enlist in the army. The battle was the last major battle of General Washington's winter in the New Jersey campaign.

After the battle at Princeton, Cornwallis abandoned many of his posts in New Jersey and ordered his army to retreat to New Brunswick.

A civilian eyewitness writer of *A Brief Narrative of the Ravages of the British and Hessians at Princeton in 1776–77* wrote that twenty-four British soldiers were found dead on the field. Varnum L. Collins recorded that George Washington claimed that the British had more than one hundred killed and three hundred captured.

There have been many conflicting records concerning the casualties, for General Washington reported that his own army had seven officers and thirty enlisted men killed. The *New York Gazette and Weekly Mercury*, the Loyalist newspaper, reported on January 17, 1777, via Yarnum Collins that "American losses at Princeton had been 400 killed and wounded."

The Battle of Bennington, 1777

The state of New Hampshire claimed the right to participate in the glory of the Battle of Bennington, Vermont, which was fought on August 16, 1777. The claim lies in the fact that the American troops were commanded by General John Stark of Manchester and that a large part of the American army was made up of New Hampshire troops. This particular battle was part of the Saratoga Campaign, which took place in Walloomsac, New York, about ten miles from its namesake, Bennington, Vermont.

New Hampshire's force of two thousand troops, reinforced by troops commanded by Colonel Seth Warner and members of the Green Mountain Boys, defeated a detachment of General John Burgoyne's army led by Lieutenant Colonel Friedrich Baum.

The battle was an extremely important victory for the rebel cause, as it reduced Burgoyne's army in size by about one thousand troops, and this led his Indian support to abandon him and deprived him of needed supplies. All of this contributed to Burgoyne's eventual surrender at Saratoga. In many ways, the victory of the Battle of Bennington galvanized colonial support for the independence movement and possibly encouraged the French to take the side of America in the effort.

Concerning the battle tactics at Bennington, on the afternoon of August 16, the weather was clear, and General Stark ordered his troops to be ready

The battlefield at Bennington, Vermont. *From Hobart Pillsbury's* New Hampshire: A History.

to attack. "There are your enemies, the Red Coats and the Tories. They are ours, or this night Molly Stark sleeps a widow." Upon hearing that the militia had melted away into the woods, General Baum assumed that the Americans were retreating. However, General Stark decided to capitalize on the weaknesses in the German officer's widely disturbed position and sent sizeable flanking parties to either side of his line. These movements were assisted by trickery employed by Stark's men that enabled them to reach safety and get closer without alarming the enemy. The Germans, most of whom spoke no English, had been informed that soldiers with bits of white paper in their hats were Loyalists and should not be fired on; Stark's men had also heard this, and many of them had suitably adorned white paper on their hats.

When the battle began at 3:00 p.m., the German position was immediately surrounded by gunfire; General Stark described it as "the hottest engagement I have every witnessed, resembling a continual clap of thunder." The enemy was properly overrun, causing many of them to surrender or escape. This left Baum and his Brunswick dragoons trapped on the high ground. The Germans fought valiantly, even though they were running low on energy and even after the destruction of their ammunition wagon. In desperation, the dragoons led a charge in an attempt to break through the opposing forces. Baum was mortally wounded in this final charge, and the remaining Germans surrender.

At the conclusion of the battle, while Stark's militiamen were busy disarming the prisoners and looting their supplies, General Heinrich von Breymann arrived with reinforcements. Seeing the Americans in disarray, he made an immediate attack. Hastily, Stark's forces regrouped and desperately tried to hold their ground against the new German attack; however, they fell back. Minutes before their lines collapsed, American troops arrived to reinforce Stark's troops. Breymann began to retreat; he had lost one quarter of his force and all his artillery pieces.

At the close of the battle, the total German and British losses at Bennington were recorded at 207 dead and 700 captured. American losses included 30 dead and 40 wounded. The prisoners were eventually marched to Boston. (One mistaken notion was that the battle was associated with the historic contest over the land grants of the State of New Hampshire in Vermont, as well as over the fiercely contested question of the jurisdiction of New York State. However, I maintain that the battle was purely a Revolutionary struggle and was caused by the capture of Fort Ticonderoga on July 6, 1777.)

After the Battle at Bennington, the British troops met with continued challenges from the Patriots. Two battles were fought at Saratoga, New York (September 19 and October 7, 1777), in which General Burgoyne's British army was defeated and about six thousand of his troops were captured; his total losses at Bennington and Saratoga reached ten thousand troops.

It is interesting to note that one of his regiments was commanded by Colonel Daniel Moore of Londonderry, son of John Moore, an early settler in the province. Captain John Wheelock, a member of Colonel Bellows's regiment in this campaign, was the son of Dr. John Wheelock, founder of Dartmouth College in Hanover. Captain Wheelock was a member of the first class of graduates of Dartmouth in 1771, and he succeeded his father as president of Dartmouth College in 1779. Another regiment commander was Captain Nicholas Gilman of Exeter. He was the son of Nicholas Gilman and brother of John Taylor Gilman, who became governor of New Hampshire. Governor Gilman served four terms as a representative and two as a senator in Congress after the Revolution.

The Battles of Saratoga, 1777

The Battles of Saratoga (September 19 and October 7, 1777) undoubtedly decided the fate of British general John Burgoyne's army in the war for independence. Many historians believe that these battles were turning points in the war.

Burgoyne's campaign to divide New England from the southern colonies had started well, but logistical problems slowed his progress. He won a small

Freeman's Farm. The clash at Freeman's Farm, September 19, 1776. *American Heritage Company.*

tactical victory over General Gates and the Continental army in the Battle of Freeman's Farm on September 19. When he again attacked the Americans in the Battle of Bemis Heights on October 7, the Americans captured a portion of the British defenses. Burgoyne was therefore compelled to retreat, and his army was surrounded by the larger American force at Saratoga, forcing him into surrender of October 17, 1777. (Formal participation by France changed the war to a global conflict. This battle also resulted in Spain contributing to the war on the American side.)

The first Battle of Saratoga (September 19) began when General Burgoyne moved some of his troops in order to flank the American position on Bemis Heights. It was Benedict Arnold who anticipated the maneuver, placing many of his troops to intercept his movement. Skirmishes continued during the following battle, while Burgoyne waited, hoping that reinforcements would arrive from New York City. Meanwhile, militia forces continued to arrive and assist the American army.

Disputes within the American camp led General Gates to strip Benedict Arnold of his command. According to Hoffman Nickerson's *The Turning Point of the Revolution*:

> Gates, following the removal of Arnold from field command, assumed command of the American left and gave him right to General Lincoln. When American scouts brought the news of Burgoyne's movement to Gates,

he ordered Morgan's riflemen out of the far left, with Poor's men (1ˢᵗ, 2ⁿᵈ, and 3ʳᵈ New Hampshire) on the left; the 2ⁿᵈ and 4ᵗʰ New York Regiments on the right; and Learned's (1ˢᵗ New York, 1ˢᵗ Canadian, 2ⁿᵈ, 8ᵗʰ and 9ᵗʰ Massachusetts regiments, plus militia companies) in the center. A force of 1,200 New York militia under brigadier General Abraham Broeck was held in reserve behind Learned's line.

More than 8,000 Americans took the field that day, including 1,400 troops from Benjamin Lincoln's command who were deployed when the action became fierce.

While the first battle was in progress, American troops also attacked British positions in the location of Fort Ticonderoga by bombarding the fort for several days before withdrawing. British general Henry Clinton captured American forts in the Hudson River highlands on October 6, but his efforts were fruitless—he was too late to assist General Burgoyne, who attacked Bemis Heights again on the seventh after he knew that he was not going to receive aid in time. However, in defiance of orders to stay off the battlefield, General Arnold rallied the American troops and forced Burgoyne back to the position he had held before the September 19 battle. The Americans also captured a portion of the British defenses.

After both battles at Saratoga, General Burgoyne had lost about one thousand men, leaving him outnumbered by three to one, while American losses came to about five hundred killed and wounded. By October 13, Burgoyne was surrounded at Saratoga, and on October 17, he surrendered his army. The remnants of his expedition retreated from Ticonderoga back to Quebec.

The British had learned that the Americans would fight. Said one British officer, "The courage and obstinacy with which the Americans fought were the astonishment of everyone, and more became fully convinced that they are not the contemptible enemy we had hitherto imagined them, incapable of standing a regular engagement, and that they would only fight behind strong and powerful works."

The Battle of Monmouth, June 28, 1778

The Battle of Monmouth (or Battle of Monmouth Courthouse) was fought in Monmouth County, New Jersey. The Continental army, commanded by General George Washington, attacked the rear of the

British column commanded by Lieutenant General Henry Clinton as they left Monmouth Courthouse.

It was Major General Charles Lee who had allowed the British rearguard commander Lieutenant General Cornwallis to seize the initiative; however, General Washington's timely arrival on the battlefield rallied the Americans along a hilltop hedgerow.

Cornwallis pressed his attack and captured the hedgerow. Washington consolidated his troops in a new line on the heights behind marshy ground, used his artillery to fix the British in their position and then brought up a four-gun battery under Major General Nathanael Greene on nearby Combs Hill to enfilade the British line, requiring Cornwallis to withdraw his troops.

Finally, General Washington tried to hit the British rear guard on both flanks, but the darkness of the evening ended the engagement. Both armies held the field; however, the British commander General Clinton withdrew his troops undetected during the evening (at midnight) to resume his army's march to New York City.

The battle demonstrated the increasing effectiveness of Washington's army after its six months' encampment at Valley Forge, where constant drilling under officers such as Major General Friedrich Wilhelm von Steuben, Major General Gilbert du Motier and Marquis de Lafayette greatly improved the army's discipline and its much-needed morale. The battle improved the military reputations of General Washington, Marquis de Lafayette and Anthony Wayne but ended the career of Charles Lee, who would face court-martial for his failures that day. Lee was court-martialed at

General Washington and Von Steuben inspecting the troops. *Grange Collection, New York.*

George Washington and his wife at Valley Forge. *From Hobart Pillsbury's* New Hampshire: A History.

the Village Inn at Englishtown, where he was found guilty and relieved of his command for one year.

According to John Ferling's *Almost a Miracle*, "After the battle, the British continued their march eastwards until they reached Sandy Hook. From there they were taken by boat to New York City where they began preparing the city's defenses in expectation of an attack. Charles Hector d'Estaing's fleet arrived just too late, narrowly missing a chance to trap Clinton's army at Sandy Hook."

The plans to attack New York were abandoned, and it remained the major base for the British forces until 1783. Monmouth was the last major battle in the North and the largest one-day battle of the Revolution when measured in terms of participation. (The Monmouth Battlefield is one of the best-preserved battlefields from the Revolutionary War. During the month of June each year, the Battle of Monmouth is reenacted at Monmouth Battlefield State Park in modern Freehold Township and Manalapan.)

The Battle of Stony Point, July 16, 1779

The Battle of Stony Point took place on July 16, 1779, in a well-planned evening attack under a selected group of General Washington's Continental army under the command of General Wayne. General Wayne defeated the

British troops in a quick but daring assault on their outpost in Stony Point, New York. Consequently, the British troops suffered heavy losses, and this victory further boosted the morale of the Continental army. This crossing was the site used later in the war by units of the Continental army to cross the Hudson River on their way to victory over the British.

Historian Henry P. Johnston noted in *The Storming of Stony Point on the Hudson*:

> *While the strategic value of capturing Stony Point was up for debate, it was regardless a huge victory for morale for the Continental Army. Its minimal strategic value was that it asserted Washington's foothold on the nearby West Point. Washington visited the battle site on the 17th of July, and applauded the men responsible for its capture after viewing the harsh terrain that was traversed by the assaulting forces.*

The Stony Point State Historic Site preserved the battlefield, where tours and demonstrations are presented during the summer season. There is a museum on the site that features artifacts from the battle. The site was designated a National Historic Landmark 1961 and was listed on the National Register of Historic Places in 1966. The battlefield features historic markers that commemorate specific sights and location of important battles at the fortress.

VICTORY IS IN SIGHT

By the close of the war in 1780, most of the battles had been concentrated to the southern states. The British took Charleston, South Carolina, and Lord Cornwallis held the city. New Hampshire put three regiments into the field for duty at West Point, New York. Later, the New Hampshire regiments moved to New Jersey, where General Poor was killed in a duel with a French officer. The regiments in that campaign were commanded by Colonels Joseph Cilley, George Reed and Alexander Scammell. Two other regiments were raised for the defense of West Point, under Colonel Moses Nichols and Colonel Josiah Bartlett. Colonel Bartlett was a member of the Committee of Safety and resided in Nottingham.

Hobart Pillsbury recalled the closing campaigns of the war:

> *In 1780, after a winter at Morristown, which was in some respects worse than Valley Forge, the army opened up in the spring with a southern*

campaign. Part of the New Hampshire troops remained in New York, and part went to Virginia. Cornwallis was pursued by Lafayette's forces and the French fleet blockaded him at Yorktown. Here the American Army of 9,000 men and the French Army of 7,000 massed together and compelled the surrender of General Cornwallis on October 19, 1781.

Victory at Yorktown, 1781

The victory at Yorktown broke the resolve of the British government. Isolated diplomatically in Europe, stymied militarily in American and lacking public support at home, the British ministry gave up active prosecution of the war.

While criticizing these British blunders in their military leadership, historians have emphasized the high odds against British success given the broad support in America for the rebel cause. Although only one third of the white colonists were zealous Patriots, another third supported the war effort by paying taxes and joining the militia. Moreover, the Patriots had experienced politicians who commanded public support and, in George Washington, an inspired leader of the Continental army.

Digging Trenches at Yorktown. Preparation of the trenches and artillery sites for the siege of Yorktown, Virginia. *Mort Künstler.*

Finally, Washington had a greater margin from error than the British generals did because Patriots controlled local governments. Alone, the Patriot militia lacked the organization necessary to defeat the British army. However, in combination with the Continental forces, it proved potent, providing the margin of victory at Saratoga in 1777 and forcing Cornwallis from the Carolinas in 1781. In the end, the American people decided the outcome. Preferring Patriot rule, they refused to support Loyalist forces or accept occupation by the British army. Consequently, while the British won many military victories, they achieved little. Once the American rebels had the financial and military support of France, they could reasonably hope for a victory (such as that at Yorktown) that would end the conflict. Altogether, New Hampshire furnished 12,497 men for the Revolutionary War.

Peace talks in Paris (in April 1782) took two years to conclude the war. The treaty was stalled by the French and Spanish because they still hoped for a major naval or territorial conquest. Their delaying tactics infuriated American diplomats

Benjamin Franklin, John Adams and John Hay. Fearing that France might sacrifice American interests, the Patriot diplomats negotiated secretly with the British, preparing, if necessary, to sign a separate peace. The British ministry was also eager for a quick settlement because Parliament no longer supported the war and officials feared the loss of a rich West Indian sugar island.

Exploiting the rivalry between Britain and France, the American diplomats secured peace on very favorable terms. In the Treaty of Paris, signed on September 3, 1783, Great Britain formally recognized the independence of its seaboard colonies. While retaining Canada, Britain also relinquished its claims to lands south the Great Lakes and east of the Mississippi River and

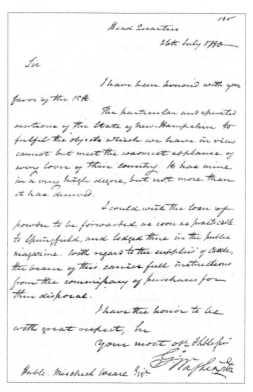

Letter from George Washington to Meshech Weare of New Hampshire. *Author's collection.*

Above, left: Letter from Cornwallis to His Excellency George Washington, 1781. *Richard T. Nowitz Collection, Simon & Schuster Children's Publishing Division.*

Above, right: King George III. *Author's collection.*

Below: Letter to Paris from King George III, Windsor Castle, London, England, November 19, 1782, 10:12 p.m.—surrender, "granting a Separation to North America." *Author's collection.*

promised to withdraw British garrisons. Leaving the pro-British Indian people in trans-Appalachian west to their fate, the British negotiators did not insist on a separate Indian territory. Only Americans profited from the treaties, which gave them independence from Britain and opened the trans-Appalachian west for settlement.

Windsor Nov. 19, 1782 10.23 PM

Mr. Townshend may send the message to Paris the draft of the Preliminary Articles and the Dispatches as soon as they are ready without waiting for my seeing the latter. He cannot be surprised at my not being over anxious for the perusal of them as Parliament having to my astonishment come into the idea of granting a Separation to North America, has disabled me from longer defending the just rights of this kingdom. But I certainly disclaim thinking myself answerable for any evils that may arise from the adoption of this measure as necessity not conviction has made me subscribe to it.

George R [ex]

A MOMENT OF PRIDE

There have been many events in New Hampshire's history, especially during the period of the Revolution, on which we may look back with pride. The following list is found in Hobart Pillsbury's *New Hampshire*:

- *New Hampshire was the first colony to commit an overt act of revolution against the government of Great Britain—the attack on Fort William and Mary in Portsmouth Harbor in 1774.*
- *New Hampshire was the first colony to declare its independence of British rule—three weeks before the Fourth of July, 1776.*
- *New Hampshire was the first State to adopt a constitution based upon the right of the people to govern themselves, a constitution adopted by delegates elected for that purpose by the people, the Constitution of 1775.*
- *New Hampshire cast the ninth and deciding vote in favor of the ratification of the Constitution of the United States.*

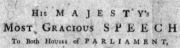

Above, left: "His Majesty's Most Gracious Speech to Both Houses of Parliament, on Friday, October 27, 1775." *Hall & Sellers.*

Above, right: A proclamation by the king of England, King George III, printed by Charles and Williams Studio. The broadside is in possession of the Boston Public Library. *Printers to the King's Most Excellent Majesty, 1775.*

Left: "An Association, proposed to the loyal citizens." The broadside is in response to General Howe's proclamation calling on Boston Tories to organize for the preservation of order and good government. This broadside is in possession of the Boston Public library. *Printers to the King's Most Excellent Majesty, 1775.*

Chapter 4

NEW HAMPSHIRE REGIMENTS AND MILITIAS

THE FIRST NEW HAMPSHIRE REGIMENT

The First New Hampshire Regiment, also known as the Fifth Continental Regiment, was called to duty on April 26, 1775—seven days after the Battles of Lexington and Concord—as the first of three Continental army regiments raised by the State of New Hampshire. The first regiment, of eight hundred troops, was commanded by New Hampshire's General John Stark and Colonel Joseph Cilley, and his adjutant was Cabel Stark, young son of General John Stark. According to historian Hobart Pillsbury:

> *This young soldier of 16 years fought at Bunker Hill and distinguished himself in the battles of Stillwater and Saratoga. The regiment saw action at Bunker Hill, the Battle of Trois-Rivieres, the Battle of Trenton, Battle of Princeton, Battle of Saratoga, Battle of Monmouth, the Battle of Stony Point, the Sullivan Expedition and the Battle of Yorktown. Both the Second and Third New Hampshire Regiments merged into the First New Hampshire Regiment during the summer of 1773. The regiment was discharged on January 1, 1784, after serving more than eight years, the longest of any American unit during the war.*

The Second New Hampshire Regiment

The Second New Hampshire Regiment, also known as the Second Continental Regiment, was the second regiment called to duty, in May 1775. Historian Pillsbury continued his account:

> *The regiment's first commander was Colonel Enoch Poor and Major Joseph Cilley. The Second Regiment saw action at the Battle of Trois-Rivieres, Battle of Trenton, Battle of Princeton, Battle of Hubbardton, the Battle of Saratoga, Battle of Monmouth, the Sullivan Expedition and the Battle of Yorktown. During the summer of 1783, the Second New Hampshire Regiment along with the Third Regiment was merged into the First New Hampshire Regiment and was discharged on January 1, 1784.*

The Third New Hampshire Regiment

The Third New Hampshire Regiment, also known as the Eighth Continental Regiment, was called to duty on June 1, 1775, as the third Continental army regiment raised by the State of New Hampshire. According to Pillsbury:

> *Its first commander was Colonel James Reed. The regiment saw action at the Battle of Bunker Hill, Battle of Trois-Rivieres, Battle of Trenton, Battle of Princeton, Battle of Saratoga, Battle of Monmouth, the Sullivan Expedition, and the Battle of Yorktown. During the summer of 1783 all three regiments merged into the First New Hampshire Regiment and was discharged on January 1, 1784.*

Additional New Hampshire Regiments

Bedel's Regiment

Bedel's regiment was raised first as a company of rangers from Coos County on May 26, 1775, under the command of Timothy Bedel. Its purpose was the protection of the Great North Woods and northern New Hampshire during the early day of the Revolution. Between the years of 1775 and 1776, eight more companies of North Country rangers were recruited as the regiment joined the Continental army. This army was involved in the Battle of Fort St. Jean and the Battle of The Cedars during the invasion of Canada. Most of the troops in the regiment were captured at The Cedars. The regiment was discharged on January 1, 1777, in Coos County, New Hampshire.

Bellows's Regiment

Bellows's regiment of militia, also known as the Sixteenth New Hampshire Militia Regiment, was called to duty at Walpole on September 21, 1777. The regiment was enlisted as reinforcement for the Continental army during the Saratoga Campaign. The regiment served in General William Whipple's brigade of the New Hampshire militia. After the surrender of Burgoyne's army on October 17, the regiment was discharged on October 27, 1777.

Chase's Regiment

Chase's regiment of militia, also known as the Thirteenth New Hampshire Militia Regiment, was called to duty at Cornish on September 22, 1777. The regiment was enlisted as reinforcement for the Continental army during the Saratoga Campaign. Later, the regiment joined forces with General Horatio Gates in the British engagement with General John Burgoyne in northern New York. The regiment also served with General William Whipple's brigade. After the surrender of Burgoyne's army on October 17, the regiment was discharged on October 24, 1777.

Drake's Regiment

Drake's regiment of militia, also known as the Second New Hampshire Militia Regiment, was called to duty at Portsmouth on September 8, 1777. As with Bellows's and Chase's regiments, they were called up as reinforcements for the Continental army during the Saratoga Campaign, and they likewise joined forces with Chase's regiment in New York, and with General Horatio Gates as he and his men faced the British forces. With the surrender of Burgoyne's army on October 17, the regiment was discharged on December 15, 1777.

Evans's Regiment

Evans's regiment of militia, also known as the Fourth New Hampshire Militia Regiment, was called to duty at Exeter on September 8, 1777. It, too, was engaged to act as reinforcement for the Continental army during the Saratoga Campaign. Immediately after the campaign, it joined forces with General Horatio Gates as he and his men faced the British in New York. After the surrender of Burgoyne's army on October 17, the regiment was discharged on December 15, 1777.

Hobart's Regiment

Hobart's regiment of militia, also known as the Twelfth New Hampshire Militia Regiment, was called to duty on July 21, 1777, at Plymouth for General Stark's Brigade at Charlestown, New Hampshire, during the Saratoga Campaign. Hobart's regiment made an assault on Friedrich Baum and his men during the Battle of Bennington as Moses Nichols attacked from the rear and Benjamin Simonds attacked from the south. Hobart's regiment continued along with Stark's Brigade to cut off British general John Burgoyne from retreat after the Battle of Freeman's Farm. The regiment was discharged on October 26, 1777.

Long's Regiment

Long's regiment was raised on May 14, 1776, at New Castle under the command of Colonel Pierce Long for service with the Continental army. The regiment was stationed at Fort Ticonderoga and Mount Independence on Lake Chaplain and saw action at Fort Ann, New York, on July 6, 1777, against General Burgoyne's army. The regiment was discharged in July 1777.

Moore's Regiment

Moore's regiment of militia, also known as the Ninth New Hampshire Militia Regiment, was called up at on September 29, 1777, at Lydeborough under the command of General William Whipple. The regiment was engaged as reinforcement for the Continental army during the Saratoga Campaign. With the surrender of Burgoyne's army on October 17, the regiment was discharged on October 27, 1777. General John Stark gave the regiment a brass four-pound cannon that had captured at the Battle of Bennington, Vermont.

Moulton's Regiment

Moulton's regiment of militia, also known as the Third Regiment of New Hampshire Militia, was called to duty in April 1775 at Hampton under the command of Colonel Jonathan Moulton. The regiment conducted a twenty-four-hour lookout at Little Boar's Head in North Hampton, where all the coastal shipping could be watched and a warning could be given to the local areas in the event of an attack. Colonel Moulton led the regiment during the Saratoga Campaign alongside General Stark in northern New York. For the remainder of the war, the regiment spent its remaining time guarding the seacoast of New Hampshire.

Nichols's Regiment

Nichols's regiment of militia, also known as the Fifth New Hampshire Militia Regiment, was called to duty on July 21, 1777, at Winchester for General Stark's Brigade at Charlestown, New Hampshire, during the Saratoga Campaign. Nichols's regiment saw action at the Battle of Bennington and continued service in Stark's Brigade to cut off the British from retreat or supply after the Battle of Freeman's Farm. Nichols's regiment also participated in General John Sullivan's campaign in Rhode Island on August 29, 1778. The regiment was discharged on January 1, 1779.

Stickney's Regiment

Stickney's regiment of militia, also known as the Eleventh New Hampshire Militia Regiment was called to duty on July 21, 1777, at Pembroke for General John Stark's Brigade at Charlestown, New Hampshire, during the Saratoga Campaign. A part of Stickney's regiment was sent to Otter Creek on August 4 to clean out any remaining Loyalists. On August 16, 1777, Stickney's regiment and Hobart's regiment made the major attack on Friedrich Baum's redoubt during the Battle of Bennington, as Moses Nichols attacked from the rear and Benjamin Simonds attacked from the south. Lieutenant Colonel Nathaniel Emerson's detachment arrived along with Seth Warner's Green Mountain Boys in time to cut off Heinrich von Breymann's reinforcements. Stickney's regiment continued on with Stark's Brigade to cut off British general John Burgoyne from retreat after the Battle of Freeman's Farm. The regiment was discharged on October 26, 1777.

Whitcomb's Rangers

Whitcomb's Rangers were called to duty on October 15, 1776, at Fort Ticonderoga in New York. They consisted of two companies of New Hampshire rangers in service with the Continental army under the command of Benjamin Whitcomb, a veteran of Bedel's regiment. The rangers saw action at the Battle of Hubbardton, the Battle of Bennington and the Battle of Saratoga. They were discharged on January 1, 1781.

Reorganization of the Army, 1779–80

There was no question that New Hampshire had its quota—three "regular" Continental regiments—in the service of the country. On October 3 and 21, Congress resolved to reorganize the army, to take effect on January 1, 1781. By the same resolution, New Hampshire's quota was reduced to two regiments. Hobart Pillsbury noted in *New Hampshire*:

> *Accordingly, on January 1, 1781, under General Washington's general order, dated Army headquarters, Totoway, November 1, 1780, the three regiments of New Hampshire were reduced to two, and Colonel Joseph Cilley, of the First New Hampshire, was retired and succeeded by Colonel Alexander Scammell, of the Third Regiment, whose officers had become supernumerary by its abolishment.*
>
> *In like manner, by resolution of Congress, another consolidation took place January 1, 1783, and the Second Regiment was disbanded and consolidated into the ranks of the First.*
>
> *On November 3, 1783, all of the Continental Army was disbanded, except such as General Washington especially designated to remain in the service. The First New Hampshire was especially honored by the commander-in-chief and I took part in the ceremonies in New York attending the evacuation of the British Army, November 25, 1783. It then returned to duty at West Point.*

The last official act of General Washington before the resignation of his commission was to designate what troops should be retained after January 1, 1784. Accordingly, Major General Henry Knox—in a General Order dated by Army Headquarters to be West Point on December 23, 1783—designated a small artillery force and detachment from the Massachusetts line, together with Captain James Frye's and Captain Cole Porter's companies of the First New Hampshire, to maintain in the service.

Hobart Pillsbury continued:

These two companies and the Massachusetts companies were organized into a regiment, under command of Colonel Henry Jackson, constituting the Fourth Massachusetts Continental Infantry. Thus the First New Hampshire ceased to exist, after a continuous service of eight years and eight months. The two companies remained in the service five months longer, until June 22, 1784, when they, with the rest of the army, were honorably discharged. It is gratifying to every son and daughter of New Hampshire to know that the First Regiment, commanded by Stark at Bunker Hill, Cilley at Saratoga, and Scammell at Yorktown, received the distinction of being especially designated by Washington to be retained in service of any regiment in the Continental Army, that is, nine years and one month.

Naval Operations in the Revolutionary War

During the war, the New Hampshire naval operations were quite important to the war department of the new nation because America did not have a navy. Privateers were fitted out at Portsmouth, patrolled the Atlantic Ocean and penetrated into the edge of Arctic Ocean in search of British ships.

Naval battles on the high seas were fought with cannons of different sizes. These projectiles fired not only solid cannonballs but also chain shot, which consisted of two halves of cannonballs linked together by a chain, used to sever the enemy's rigging. Grapeshot, which fired loads of musket balls to attack the ship's crew, was also used.

Early in the war, the celebrated and most respected naval commander John Paul Jones sailed from Portsmouth in the *Ranger*, a privateer of that port, destined to act against the British commerce. Hobart Pillsbury noted:

He landed both in England and Scotland, and plundered the house of the Earl of Selkirk. After landing his plunder in France, he again put to sea and sailed to the Irish coast. Having learned that the British ship of war "Drake" was then lying in Waterford Harbor, he sent to her captain a challenge for a combat, which was accepted. The ships met and fought—

after an action of an hour and a quarter, the "Drake," having had 180 of her men killed and wounded, struck her colors to the "Ranger."

The loss on the American vessel was only twenty men. After this victory, John Paul Jones left the *Ranger* for another vessel, the *Bonhomme Richard*, in which his exploits rendered him the terror of the British seas.

During the Revolution, the navy used the first experimental submarine. This was a new concept of an underwater vessel. The first of these vessels was called the *Turtle*, and it was invented by David Bushnell for the purpose of attaching explosives to British ships without them knowing it. The submarine *Turtle* was launched on September 6, 1776, for the sole purpose of drilling a screw into the British ship HMS *Eagle*. This venture proved to be unsuccessful, failed to secure the explosive and was forced to retreat. Further attempts with the *Turtle* also failed.

Tories: Royalists in New Hampshire

The following summary of New Hampshire Tories was written during the Revolutionary period. No sketch would be complete without the following account of those people living in the Granite State who did not join in the American Revolution. The statement about the treatment of the Tories is presented by historian Pillsbury in *New Hampshire*:

In March 1776, Congress deemed necessary to ascertain the extent of Royalism in the colonies, and recommended that a test be submitted to the people. It was considered that those who signed it could be depended upon to support the Revolutionary movement, and those who did not sign it were to be disarmed and so made for a time incapable of effective opposition. This pledge was called the Association Test, and the text was as follows:

> *We, the Subscribers, do hereby solemnly engage and promise that we will to the utmost of*
> *Our power, at the Risque of our Lives and Fortunes, with Arms oppose the Hostile Proceed—*
> *ings of the British Fleets and Armies, against the United American Colonies.*

By request of Congress, this was presented for signature to all males above twenty-one years of age, except lunatics, idiots and "negroes."

The 87 towns from which the Association Test returns have been preserved in the archives represented a total of 50,682 of population, or bear the signatures of 8,567 men, and the names of 781 who did not sign. One hundred and thirty-one of these refused because of religious scruples, conscience, or other reasons not hostile to the cause of the colonies, and four were reported absent, leaving 646, or 6.9 percent of possible signers who refused to sign without apparent reason other than an unwillingness to support the war.

In Acworth, Antrim, Atkinson, Barnstead, Bow, Brookline, Canaan, Candia, Canterbury, Chester, Concord, Dublin, Effingham, Enfield, Gilsum, Lebanon, Lempster, Loudon, Manchester, Meredith, Newport, North Hampton, Peterborough, Piermont, Rindge, Rye, Seabrook, Sunapee, Surry, Wakefield, 31 towns, all signed.

July 19, 1777, the House of Representatives appointed a committee to report some method for taking firearms from such persons in the State that refused to take up arms against the enemies of the American States. The same day the committee recommended that the colonels of the several regiments of militia be empowered to disarm the disaffected persons, and the arms so taken be appraised by two disinterested men, and be paid for unless returned. The recommendation was adopted, but we find no record of further action on this plan, although here and there a few Royalists were disarmed by local committees of safety.

August 28, 1777, the Federal Congress states that there was reason to believe that Quakers in different States were carrying on a treasonable correspondence, and recommended that the States investigate the matter by seizing and examining their records and papers, and that any documents of a political nature so found be forwarded to Congress. November 8 following, the New Hampshire House of Representatives appoint a committee to apply to clerks of the Quaker societies in Dover, Hampton Falls, Seabrook, Brentwood, Weare, and other towns for the privilege of examining their records, and gave the committee power to break and enter in case access was refused. There is no evidence on record that any incriminating documents were found among the Quakers of New Hampshire.

The Proscription Act, or Act of Banishment, was passed November 19, 1778, and bore the title "An act to prevent the return to this State of certain persons therein named, and of others who have left or shall leave this State, or either of the United States of America, and have joined or shall join the enemies thereof."

Seventy-six men are named in the act, the first of whom was Governor John Wentworth. According to Pillsbury:

[T]hey are described as having left this State and joined the enemies, thereby not only basely deserting the cause of liberty and depriving these States of

their personal services at a time when they ought to have afforded their utmost assistance in defending the same against the invasions of a cruel enemy, but abetting the cause of tyranny, and manifesting an inimical disposition to said States, and a design to aid the enemies thereof in their wicked purposes.

In this list we find 30 "Esquires" or gentlemen (using social distinctions of that time rather than this), 1 military officer, 5 mariners, 4 physicians, 8 merchants, 5 traders, 19 yeomen or farmers, 1 rope-maker, 1 post-rider, 1 printer, and 1 clerk or minister. Thirty-three of these were citizens of Portsmouth; Londonderry and Dunbarton had 6 each, Keene 5, Charlestown, 4, Hollis 3, Newmarket, Amherst, Alstead and Hindale 4 each, and Pembroke, Exeter, Concord, Merrimack, New Ipswich, Francestown, Peterborough, Nelson, Winchester, Rindge, and Claremont 1 each. The penalty provided in the act for a voluntary return to the State was for a first offense transportation to British territory, and for a second offense death.

The Confiscation Act followed eight days later on November 28, 1778, and in it were named twenty-five of those included in the Proscription Act, as well as three others not previously mentioned. They were described as men who have

since the commencement of hostilities between Great Britain and the United States of America, left this and the other United States, and gone over to and joined the enemy thereof, and have, to the utmost of their power, aided, abetted, and assisted the said enemy in their cruel designs of wresting from the good people of said States their Liberty, civil and religious, and of taking from them their property, and converting the same to the use of their said enemy.

All their property in New Hampshire was declared forfeited to the use of the state:

The first man in New Hampshire to suffer for his suspected Royalist tendencies was Benjamin Thompson of Concord, afterwards Count Rumford. In the summer of 1774 he was summoned before a committee of the citizens of Concord on the charge of being unfriendly to American liberty. No proof was found, he denied the accusation, and was discharged. But the hostility of his neighbors continued to increase, and in November, by the advice and assistance of his brother-in-law, Judge Timothy Walker, left his wife and child and secretly went back to Woburn. He was arrested there May 15, 1775, on the same indefinite charges. Again no proof was produced, and he was discharged.

Chapter 5

DISTINGUISHED PATRIOTS OF THE REVOLUTIONARY WAR

NEW HAMPSHIRE SIGNERS OF THE DECLARATION OF INDEPENDENCE

Josiah Bartlett

Dr. Bartlett of Kingston served on the Committee of Safety. Before the war, he provided his attic for secret militia meetings. Later, Dr. Bartlett served in the convention to ratify the United States Constitution and in 1790 as president of New Hampshire. When the term "president" was changed in 1792, Bartlett became our state's first governor. Dr. Josiah Bartlett was also a revolutionary in his profession.

Matthew Thornton

Mr. Thornton was born in Ireland and immigrated to Maine with his family. He grew up in Worcester, Massachusetts, where he studied medicine and became a doctor. Later, Dr. Thornton moved to Londonderry, New Hampshire, when he was ready to start his own practice.

Under the royal government, Dr. Thornton was a colonel in the Londonderry militia. Governor Wentworth rewarded his services by giving his family a northern township known today as Thornton.

Matthew Thornton was one of the first citizens to urge complete independence from Great Britain. He took part in the Provincial Congress from its beginning and was president of the Fourth and Fifth Congresses. He chaired the committee that wrote the New Hampshire Constitution in 1776 and remained active in New Hampshire and in Philadelphia in the Continental Congress.

William Whipple Jr.

William Whipple Jr. was born at Kittery, Maine, and was educated at a common school to study how to be a merchant, a judge and a soldier until he went to sea. Later, he became a ship's master. In 1759, he landed in Portsmouth, New Hampshire, and established himself as a merchant in partnership with his brother. Whipple and his family lived in the historic Moffatt-Ladd House on Market Street in Portsmouth.

In 1775, Whipple was elected to represent his town at the Provincial Congress. In 1776, New Hampshire dissolved the royal government and recognized a House of Representatives and an Executive Council. Whipple became a council member and a member of the Committee of Safety and was elected to the Continental Congress, serving through 1779.

In 1777, he was made a brigadier general of the New Hampshire militia, participating in the expedition against General Burgoyne at the Battles of Stillwater and Saratoga, raising and commanding a brigade (Ninth, Tenth, Thirteenth and Sixteenth Regiments) of New Hampshire militia during the campaign. In 1778, General Whipple led another New Hampshire militia brigade at the Battle of Rhode Island.

After the war, General Whipple became an associate justice of the Supreme Court of New Hampshire. He suffered from a heart ailment and died on November 28, 1785.

New Hampshire Men of the Continental Army

Timothy Bedel, 1737–1787

Timothy Bedel was born in Salem, New Hampshire, and served as a lieutenant in the New Hampshire Provincial Regiment at Fort Number 4, Crown Point and Fortress Louisbourg during the French and Indian War.

According to the *Illustrated Historical and Biographical Records of the State of New Hampshire*, on May 26, 1775, during the American Revolution, Bedel was appointed to command a company of rangers to be raised at Coos, New Hampshire. Coos was a military command located in Haverhill.

Bedel's regiment recruited a unit that grew into a regiment of eight companies. Bedel's ranger regiment joined the Continental army during the invasion of Canada after many encounters and battles, serving with distinction.

Bedel later served as a first lieutenant in a militia regiment at the Battle of Bennington under the command of General John Stark, became a staff officer for Generals Philip Schuyler and Horatio Gates at Saratoga for Indian affairs and soon was restored to regimental command. On December 11, 1779, General Washington ordered Colonel Bedel to raise another regiment at Coos in the construction of a possible invasion route to Canada.

Some early historians believed that Bedel became a general in the New Hampshire, Vermont or New York militia. However, historian Albert Batchellor could not find any evidence of this claim because Bedel was always addressed by his contemporaries as "Colonel."

Henry Dearborn, 1751–1829

Henry Dearborn was distinguished as an American physician, a statesman and a veteran in both the American Revolutionary War and the War of 1812. Dearborn led a New Hampshire militia of sixty troops to Boston as a captain in Colonel Stark's First New Hampshire Regiment. His journal records that he was captured on December 31, 1775, during the Battle of Quebec and kept as a prisoner for one year. He was released on parole in May 1776 but was not exchanged until March 1777.

According to the *Illustrated Historical and Biographical Record of the State of New Hampshire*, after fighting at Ticonderoga, Freeman's Farm and Saratoga, Dearborn joined George Washington's main army as a lieutenant colonel at Valley Forge, where he spent the winter of 1777–78. He fought at the Battle of Monmouth in 1778, and in 1779, he accompanied Major General John Sullivan on the Sullivan Expedition against the Iroquois in upstate New York. During the winter of 1778–79, he was encamped at what is now Putnam Memorial State Park in Redding, Connecticut. Dearborn joined Washington's staff in 1781 as deputy quartermaster general with the rank of colonel, and he was present when Cornwallis surrendered after the Battle of Yorktown.

In June 1783, he was discharged from the Continental army. Later, in Massachusetts, he was promoted to the rank of brigadier general in the militia in 1787 and in 1789 to the rank of major general

Nathaniel Folsom, 1726–1790

Nathaniel Folsom lived in Exeter, New Hampshire, and joined the militia during the French and Indian War. He was a captain of a company in the New Hampshire Provincial Regiment during the Crown Point expedition, which was commanded by Sir William Johnson in 1755. During the Battle of Lake George, his company, with the aid and support from the Massachusetts artillery, captured Baron de Dieskau, the French commander in chief.

Nathaniel Folsom was elevated to the rank of colonel in the militia; however, his formal commission was revoked by Governor Wentworth after the raid on Fort William and Mary in December 1774. Colonel Folsom disregarded this communication, marched his regiment to Portsmouth and escorted the captured cannons safely back to Durham.

According to Charles Henry Bell's *Exeter in 1776*:

> On May 29, 1775, the Provincial Congress awarded him the rank of Brigadier General in command of New Hampshire's forces. This did create some confusion, for Massachusetts provincial government had named John Stark to the same position. At that time, Colonel Stark was the senior commander of the New Hampshire troops who had marched to the Siege of Boston. The confusion was resolved in June when the Continental Congress named John Sullivan General of the New Hampshire forces in the service with the Continental Army. Folsom was, however, the senior officer for militia forces within the state. Later, he was promoted to the rank of Major General, and continued to recruit, train and supply the efforts throughout the Revolutionary War.

Nicholas Gilman, 1755–1814

In November 1776, a committee of the state legislature appointed Nicholas Gilman to serve as adjutant, or administrative officer, of the Third New Hampshire Regiment. Colonel Alexander Scammell, a superb combat officer, made good use of Gilman's administrative skills in creating a potent fighting force out of the limited manpower at hand—most of the men were raw recruits from around the state. In a short time, the Third New Hampshire would be recognized as one of the mainstays of General Washington's Continental army.

Due to the fact that New Hampshire lay along the major invasion route from Canada to New York, General Washington assigned the regiments to play a key role in the strategic defense of the northern states.

According to the *Biographical Directory of the United States Congress*, in the spring of 1777, Nicholas Gilman, as well as the rest of the officers and troops of the Third New Hampshire Regiment, marched to Fort Ticonderoga on Lake

Nicholas Gilman. *Philips Exeter Academy, Exeter, New Hampshire.*

Champlain to participate in an attempt by the American forces to halt the advancement of a the British army and German regulars, as well as Indian auxiliaries, under the command of General John Burgoyne. The British were smart enough to out flank the fort, but at the last minute did the garrison, including the Third Regiment, escape capture from the British during the evening hours.

The American retreat lasted through the early summer. The delay allowed time for a mass mobilization of the New England militia, including the Third New Hampshire Regiment. This also provided Major General Horatio Gates with enough time to establish new positions near Saratoga, New York, in order to block Burgoyne's further advance. General Gates had a numerical advantage to cut off the British line of withdrawal to Canada. During this campaign, Gilman was busy preparing and training Scammell's troops. After spending a winter in Valley Forge, General Washington selected Colonel Scammell to serve as the Continental army's adjutant general, Scammell made Gilman his assistant. Promotion to the rank of captain followed in June 1778.

During his tour of duty, Captain Gilman saw action in the battles near Washington's Continental army, including Monmouth and Yorktown.

In late 1783, Captain Nicholas Gilman retired from military service and returned to Exeter to resume his family's business.

John Paul Jones, 1747–1792

John Paul Jones is considered the greatest Revolutionary naval commander and founder of our nation's naval tradition.

Bob Blythe, in a National Park Service publication, noted:

> *Having long been protected by the powerful British navy, America began the Revolutionary War naval power of any kind. Congress acted quickly to convert merchant ships to ships of war and to begin building new ships for the navy. After a brief stint as second in command of the Alfred, Jones in May 1776 took command of the sloop Providence, which mounted 21 guns. Jones soon captured 16 British vessels on a single cruise.*
>
> *Promoted to the rank of captain, Jones took command of the Alfred and soon had more prizes. In April 1778, as captain of the Ranger, he was cruising the waters close to Britain.*
>
> *Jones's greatest victory came in September 1779. He now commanded a fleet of five ships. His flagship, a 40-gun frigate, was a converted French merchant ship. Jones re-named it the Bonhomme Richard.*

On September 23, 1779, Jones encountered British merchantmen convoyed by the frigate *Serapis* and a smaller warship. Despite the superiority of the *Serapis*, Captain Jones went into action.

John Paul Jones began his naval career by hoisting our first national flag (the Grand Union flag). It was the first time it was ever hoisted on board the first ship of the Continental navy, the *Alfred*, lying off Philadelphia in the Delaware River; Jones had been ordered to the ship as first lieutenant. Jones hoisted this flag about one month before it was hoisted by General Washington, commander in chief of the Continental army, over his headquarters at Prospect Hill on January 2, 1776, at the siege of Boston.

Jones took part in several gallant actions in the early stages of the war off the North American continent. On May 10, 1777, he was ordered to his first command, the *Providence*. Later, he commanded a squadron with the *Alfred* as

John Paul Jones aboard his ship, the *Ranger. From Hobart Pillsbury's* New Hampshire: A History.

his flagship. On June 14, 1777, Congress appointed Jones to command the *Ranger*, built at Portsmouth, New Hampshire.

According to the National Park Service publication, "The first recognition of the American flag by a foreign government occurred in Quiberon Bay, France, on February, 1778, when Vice Admiral La Motte Picquet, Commander of the French fleet, returned the *Ranger's* salute of 13 gun with 9 guns."

Following this, Jones conceived the bold plan for an invasion of England and raids on the coasts in order to bring the war home to the British, with the hope that their naval forces off the North American shores would be forced to withdraw, thus relieving the pressure against Washington's sea supply line. He sailed from Brest on April 11 and boldly headed for the Irish Sea, taking prizes en route. On April 22, the *Ranger* landed at Whitehaven, spiked the guns at the fort and set fire to ships.

The National Park Service publication continued:

On September 23, 1779, John Paul Jones rose to supreme distinguish. Sighting the Superior British frigate Serapis convoying a fleet of forty-odd merchant ships around Flamborough Head, Jones stood directly for her engaged as soon as possible. He captured his opponent after his own vessel had been practically shot out from under him and she later sank, despite the pumps and every effort to save her.

This action beginning at sunset, with the full moon just rising, lasted nearly four hours, the two vessels being lashed together, starboard side to starboard side. Not only was it the most brilliant sea fight of the war, but one of the most remarkable single ship actions in history. Finally, with the Bon Homme Richard's hull of the vessel was filled with 4 to 5 feet water, gaining despite the pumps, in inking conditions; with all her guns out of action except 3 nine-pounders; with her hull holed in many places and decks all but shot away, with half of the crew killed or wounded, including several officers; with fire raging in many places and fast approaching the magazines, unchecked, the British captain asked if Jones was ready to surrender. Immediately, had his reply twofold over the roar of the battle as Jones and his men boarded the Serapis shouting his immortal words: "Surrender? I have not yet begun to fight!"

After the war ended, our government appointed Jones as its agent aboard to negotiate and settle the prize money claims; doing so, he acted as a diplomat. He was partially successful. On July 18, 1792, he died at the age of forty-five.

According to the National Park Service:

In 1899, General Porter (a graduate of the West Point Military Academy), our ambassador to France, began a diligent and tireless search for John Paul Jones's lost and forgotten grave. He was aided by the French government and in 1905 the undertaking ended in success. The body had been wonderfully preserved and positive identification was possible. A squadron of United States warships was sent to bring the hero to Annapolis and on July 6 (his birthday) 1905, John Paul Jones passed once again in triumph through the streets of Paris with French and America military escort. On April 24, 1906, commemorative services were held in Dahlgren Hall at the United State Naval Academy, participated in by President Theodore Roosevelt, the French Ambassador, other high civil military representatives, and twelve thousand people.

The following inscription is written in the marble floor on the front of sarcophagus:

JOHN PAUL JONES, 1747–1792; U.S. NAVY, 1775–1783. HE GAVE OUR NAVY ITS EARLIEST TRADITIONS OF HEROISM AND VICTORY. ERECTED BY THE CONGRESS, A.D. 1912.

The assembled Congress sitting in New York, 16 October 1787, voted unanimously to award John Paul Jones a gold medal. He was the only naval officer of out Continental Navy to be so honored.

Nathaniel Meserve, 1704–1758

Meserve was born in Portsmouth, New Hampshire, and in 1749, he was hired by the Royal Navy to build a fifty-gun warship, HMS *America*, at his shipyard. During King George's War, Nathaniel Meserve was commissioned a lieutenant colonel in the New Hampshire Militia Regiment at the 1745 capture of Fortress Louisbourg on Cape Breton Island. During the French and Indian War, Colonel Meserve led the New Hampshire Provincial Regiment in 1756 to Fort Edwards in New York and in 1757 to garrison Halifax, Nova Scotia.

Jonathan Moulton, 1726–1787

Jonathan Moulton was born in the town of North Hampton, New Hampshire. He distinguished himself by being appointed as a captain of a ranger company in the New Hampshire militia. After his appointment, he was with the New England army that took Fortress Louisbourg from the French. For the remainder of King George's War, Captain Moulton fought against the Ossipee Indians who were allied to the French in the Lakes Region until they were killed or driven to Canada. Captain Moulton and his men ambushed six Ossipee warriors during the winter on the ice of Lake Winnipesaukee. The Treaty of Aix-la-Chapelle ended the war in 1748.

In 1754, the colonial struggle in the French and Indian War commenced. Moulton once again served as a captain in the New Hampshire militia and was also elected to the New Hampshire General Court. At the conclusion of the French and Indian War, Moulton was granted a large tract of land on the north side of Lake Winnipesaukee—known today as the town of Moultonborough (named after Jonathan Moulton), New Hampton, Tamworth, Center Harbor and Sandwich—by Governors Benning and John Wentworth.

According to the *Illustrated Historical and Biographical Record of the State of New Hampshire*, it was during the Revolutionary War that Jonathan Moulton was commissioned as the colonel of the Third New Hampshire Regiment of militia. During the first two years of the revolution, Colonel Moulton's regiment guarded the eighteen-mile seacoast of New Hampshire against British invasion. In the fall of 1777, Colonel Moulton marched his troops to the Battle of Saratoga in New York and to the defeat of Lieutenant General John Burgoyne's British army invading from Canada. Moulton was promoted to brigadier general by George Washington for his gallant service and battlefield skills.

After the war was concluded, General Moulton continued his role in the New Hampshire militia. On March 25, 1785, he was promoted to brigadier general of the First Brigade of the New Hampshire militia. General Moulton died at the age of seventy-one on September 18, 1787.

Enoch Poor, 1736–1780

Enoch Poor was born and raised in Andover, Massachusetts. In 1775, he was elected to the Provincial Assembly. The Battles of Lexington and Concord caused the Assembly to call for three regiments of militia. Enoch Poor became the colonel of the Second New Hampshire Regiment, which was stationed in Portsmouth and Exeter.

During the summer of 1775, his unit was assigned into the Continental army. Poor's unit was directed to the Northern Department to be with General Richard Montgomery during the latter's invasion of Canada. After the invasion, Poor's regiment was sent back to Fort Ticonderoga, and there the unit was renamed as the Eighth Continental Regiment and attached to General Washington's main army in December at the winter quarters near Morristown, New Jersey.

On February 21, 1777, Congress promoted Poor to brigadier general. That spring, his brigade of three New Hampshire and two New York regiments was sent back to Ticonderoga. He withdrew his assignment and joined General Horatio Gates before the Battle of Saratoga, and his brigade was expanded by the addition of two regiments of Connecticut militia. In the first engagement of Saratoga, the Battle of Freeman's Farm, General Poor's brigade was the first to come to the aid of Daniel Morgan's

Enoch Poor. *From Hobart Pillsbury's* New Hampshire: A History.

attack. The second engagement was at the Battle of Bemis Heights, and General Poor's brigade was in General Benjamin Lincoln's division.

General Poor's brigade again spent the winter with the main army at Valley Forge. His troops led the last maneuvers in the Battle of Monmouth on June 28, 1778. He accompanied General Sullivan's expedition in 1779 and also led a brigade in the victory at the Battle of Newtown.

Some sources note that Poor was shot in a duel near Hackensack, New Jersey, on September 6, 1780, and that he died two days later from his wounds and from typhus.

James Reed, 1724–1807

James Reed was born in Lunenburg, Massachusetts. During the French and Indian War, he served in Colonel Brown's Massachusetts Regiment and became a lieutenant colonel. He served at Fort Ticonderoga in both 1858 and 1859.

James Reed was the original proprietor of Monadnock Fort No. 4 (now Fitzwilliam, New Hampshire). After hearing about the Battles of Lexington and Concord, Reed gathered the local militia and marched to Boston. He was appointed colonel of the Third New Hampshire Regiment and fought with John Stark's First New Hampshire Regiment at the Battle of Bunker Hill.

On April 26, 1776, the three New Hampshire regiments of the Continental army were sent to help in the invasion of Canada under the commander of General John Sullivan. James Reed never made it to Canada, for he contracted smallpox and lost his vision, which forced him to retire from military service. James Reed was promoted to brigadier general in the Continental army, but he never served at that rank due to his failing health. James Reed died at the age of eighty-three in 1807 in Fitchburg, Massachusetts.

George Reid, 1733–1815

General Reid was born in Londonderry and faithfully served in the American Revolution for about eight years. Reid began his service as a captain under the command of John Stark at Bunker Hill and later served in the Fifth Regiment of the Continental army.

Reid saw action in the battles at Long Island, White Plains, Trenton, Germantown and Saratoga, just to name a few. During the winter of 1777, he stayed with his troops and General Washington at Valley Forge. In 1783, he commanded the First New Hampshire Regiment until it was discharged at the end of 1783. He was promoted to brigadier general in charge of the New Hampshire troops in 1785.

General George Reid. *From Hobart Pillsbury's History of New Hampshire.*

Alexander Scammell, 1747–1781

Alexander Scammell was born in the town of Mendon, Massachusetts. According to Peter J. Guthorn's *American Maps and Map Makers of the Revolution*:

> *In 1772 he went to Plymouth, New Hampshire to aid the Royal Navy in surveying timberlands. Here he was associated with Samuel Holland, an accomplished surveyor and Surveyor General of the northern District. Holland's map of New York, New Jersey and part of Pennsylvania was later published by Sayer and Bennett and was widely used by both sides during the American Revolution. Scammell himself submitted a map of Maine's pine forest in 1772. Subsequently, Scammell began to read law with John Sullivan, later General Sullivan, of Durham, New Hampshire.*

Alexander Scammell. *From Hobart Pillsbury's* New Hampshire: A History.

Historian C.E. Potter wrote the following profile of Scammell's career in *The Military History of the State of New Hampshire*:

> *With the beginning of the war, Scammell became a major in the Second New Hampshire Regiment, which was in Sullivan's Brigade, and after the Siege of Boston, he was sent to reinforce the Continental Army in the Invasion of Canada. Sullivan's forces returned to Fort Ticonderoga in mid July 1776, and by August, Scammell had been assigned as Aide-de-Camp to General Sullivan.*
>
> *In September he was ordered to assist Colonel George Reid in New York and fought at the Battle of Long Island. In October 1776 he became appointed to the post of Assistant Adjutant General for Charles Lee's Division. In November Scammell was promoted to Colonel. Then on November 11, 1776 he was given command of the Third New Hampshire Regiment.*

Scammell accompanied the First and Second Regiments under Colonel Stark south to join Washington's army. Scammell crossed the Delaware with Washington and took part in the Battle of Trenton and the Battle of Princeton.

In June 1777, the recruiting of the Third New Hampshire Regiment was completed, and within two weeks, the troops had mustered in at Fort Ticonderoga. Scammell commanded the regiment at Saratoga and distinguished himself in the Battles of Freeman's Farm and Bemis Heights.

Alexander Scammell himself recorded, "Just two days after Burgoyne's surrender the regiment moved to winter quarters at Valley Forge where I was appointed adjutant general of the Continental Army by George Washington. In October 1780 I was appointed as executioner to Major John Andre, a duty that weighed heavily on me." The result was a letter written on November 16, 1780, to Washington requesting permission to resign his post and take command of a regiment of the line.

In early 1781, Scammell was reassigned as commander of the First New Hampshire Regiment. However, on May 17, 1881, he was assigned command of a light infantry detachment, which became known as Scammell's Light Infantry; this regiment fought at the Battle of King's Bridge and was the vanguard for the army's march south to Yorktown. Once at Yorktown, the regiment was organized as part of the Second Brigade of the Light Infantry Division at Yorktown in 1781.

During his duty as colonel of the First New Hampshire Regiment, he commanded a chosen corps of light infantry during the siege of Yorktown, Virginia. Unfortunately, he was captured and later wounded. He died on October 1781 due to these wounds.

John Stark, 1728–1822

John Stark was born in Londonderry, New Hampshire. He became highly respected for his accomplishments as the "Hero of Bennington" at the Battle of Bennington in 1777.

During the French and Indian War, Stark served as a second lieutenant under Major Robert Rogers during the war. As a member of Rogers' Rangers, Lieutenant Stark gained a great deal of combat experience and military knowledge of the northern frontier of the American colonies. While serving with Rogers' Rangers in 1757, he went on a scouting mission to Fort Carillon in which the rangers were ambushed. He became second in command of the rangers but refused to accompany an attack on an Indian village and instead returned to New Hampshire and his family.

Major General John Stark, from the portrait by U.D. Tenney by order of the New Hampshire legislature, 1810. *From Hobart Pillsbury's* New Hampshire: A History.

On April 19, 1775, the Battles of Lexington and Concord signaled the beginning of the American Revolutionary War. Thus, Stark returned to military service. On April 23, 1775, John Stark accepted a commission as colonel with James Reed of the Third New Hampshire Regiment. As soon as Colonel Stark could muster his men, he marched them south to Boston to support the blockaded rebels there. He made his headquarters in the Isaac Royall House in Medford, Massachusetts.

As was noted earlier on the Battle of Bunker Hill, the Americans, fearing a British attack on their position in Cambridge and Roxbury, decided to take and hold Breed's Hill in Charlestown on a high point on the peninsula overlooking Boston Harbor. On the night of the sixteenth, American troops moved into position on the heights and began digging entrenchments. Stark and Reed's New Hampshire men arrived at the scene soon after Prescott's request. Upon their arrival, Colonel Prescott allowed Stark to deploy his men where he saw fit. After surveying the landscape, he immediately moved his men to the low ground between Mystic Beach and the hill and ordered them to fortify two rail fences by stuffing grass and straw between the rails. Stark then deployed his men behind the wall.

A large contingency of British troops advanced toward the fortifications. Stark's men waited until the advancing British troops were almost upon them and then stood up and fired their weapons as one. They killed ninety men, which broke the advance. A second advance of the British infantry was attempted, and that movement was also decimated by the minutemen. A third attempt was made, again with heavy losses to the British. The American troops soon experienced low reserves of ammunition and were forced to back off their defense. Stark directed the New Hampshire regiment's fire so as to provide some cover for Colonel Prescott's retreating troops.

The British finally took the hill that day but with heavy losses, especially among the officers. Upon the arrival of General George Washington two weeks after the battle, the siege reached a stalemate until March the following year, when cannons seized from Fort Ticonderoga were positioned on Dorchester Heights during a nighttime maneuver. This was an act of military genius, for the placement of these cannons threatened the British fleet in Boston Harbor and forced General Howe to withdraw all his forces from the Boston garrison and sail for Halifax, Nova Scotia.

General Washington knew that the British would certainly return, but to New York, and he knew that he needed experienced soldiers like Stark. He offered Stark a command in the Continental army. Stark and his New Hampshire regiment agreed to join. He and his men traveled to New Jersey to join Washington. They were with Washington in the Battles of Princeton and Trenton during the late 1776 and early 1777.

After the successful Battle at Trenton, General Washington requested that Stark return to New Hampshire to recruit more men for the Continental army. Stark agreed, but upon returning home, he learned that while fighting at Trenton, a fellow New Hampshire colonel had been promoted to brigadier general in the Continental army. On March 23, 1777, Stark resigned his commission in disgust; however, he did pledge his future support to New Hampshire if he was needed.

Four months passed, and the State of New Hampshire offered him a commission as brigadier general of the New Hampshire militia. Soon after his commission, General Stark assembled more than 1,400 militiamen. He moved to Manchester, where he was ordered by Major General Benjamin Lincoln to reinforce Philip Schuyler's Continental army on the Hudson River.

According to Mark M. Boatner III in the *Encyclopedia of the American Revolution*:

> *General Stark refused to obey, but General Lincoln understood his situation and allowed him to operate independently against the rear of General John Burgoyne's British army.*
>
> *As it happened, Burgoyne sent an expedition under Lieutenant Colonel Friedrich Baum to capture American supplies at Bennington, Vermont. Stark heard about the raid and marched his force to Bennington. Meanwhile, Baum received intelligence that Bennington was held by 1,800 men. On August 14, Baum asked Burgoyne for reinforcements but assured his army commander that his opponents would not give him much trouble. The Brunswick officer then fortified his position and waited for Lieutenant Colonel Heinrich von Breymann's 642 soldiers and two 6-pound cannons to reach him. Colonel Seth Warner also set out with his 350 men to reinforce General Stark.*
>
> *General Stark led his remaining 1,200 troops against Baum, saying, "We'll beat them before night or Molly Stark's a widow." Baum was fatally hit and his men gave up around 5:00 p.m. With Stark's men somewhat scattered by their victory, Breymann's column appeared on the scene. At this moment Colonel Seth Warner's 350 Green Mountain Boys arrived to confront Breymann's men. Between Stark and Warner, the Germans were stopped and then forced to withdraw. The New Hampshire and Vermont soldiers severely mauled Breymann's command.*
>
> *As a commander of New England militia, Stark had one rare and priceless quality; he knew the limitations of his men. They were innocent of military training, undisciplined, and unenthusiastic about getting shot. With these men he killed over 200 of Europe's vaunted regulars with a loss of 14 Americans killed.*
>
> *General Stark's action contributed to the surrender of Burgoyne's northern army after the Battle of Saratoga by raising American morale, by keeping the British from getting supplies, and by subtracting several hundred men from the enemy order of battle.*

After serving with distinction during those war years, General Stark retired to his home in Derryfield. It has been said that of all those war generals, John Stark was the only true general of distinction, for he retired from the service at the end of the war. In 1809, a group of Bennington veterans gathered to commemorate the battle. General Stark was then eighty-one and was not well enough to travel, but he sent them a letter that announced, "Live Free or Die." In 1945, this statement became New Hampshire's state motto.

John Sullivan, 1740–1795

John Sullivan, a distinguished American general during the Revolutionary War, was also a prominent delegate in the Continental Congress and a United States judge.

Born in Somersworth, John Sullivan studied law and began a practice in 1764. During the early 1700s, Sullivan became friends with the royal governor John Wentworth. As the American Revolution grew nearer, he began to become involved with the Patriot radicals. In 1774, the First Provincial Congress sent him as a delegate to the First Continental Congress. After Paul Revere alerted the Portsmouth militia of a rumored British movement toward Fort William and Mary in December 1774, John Sullivan was one of the leaders of the militia troops who raided the fort for its military provisions on December 14. In 1775, he returned to the Second Continental Congress, but when he was appointed to the rank of brigadier general in June, he left to join the army at the siege of Boston.

After the British evacuated Boston in the spring of 1776, General Washington sent General Sullivan north as commander in Quebec. He took command of the faltering invasion force and sent some of the troops on an unsuccessful counterattack against the British at Trois-Rivieres. He withdrew the survivors to Crown Point. This failed attempt with the British attack drew some controversy between Congress and General Sullivan, and members used him as a scapegoat for the failed invasion of Canada. He was exonerated and promoted to major general on August 9, 1776.

General Sullivan rejoined General Washington and was placed in command of the troops on Long Island to defend against British general Howe's forces, who surrounded New York City. On August 23, General Washington divided the command between General Sullivan and General Israel Putnam. These appointments led to some confusion as to who was in command and contributed to the American defeat at the Battle of Long Island four days later. General Sullivan showed unquestionable bravery as he engaged the Hessian troops with only a pistol in each hand. However, he was captured.

Major General John Sullivan. *From Hobart Pillsbury's* New Hampshire: A History.

According to David H. Fischer's *Washington's Crossing*:

General Howe and his brother, Admiral Richard Howe, managed to convince Sullivan that a conference with members of the Continental Congress might lead to peace, and released him on parole to deliver a message to the Congress in Philadelphia, proposing an informal meeting to discuss ending the armed conflict between Britain and its rebellious colonies.

After Sullivan's speech to Congress, John Adams spoke on this diplomatic attempt, calling General Sullivan a "decoy-duck" and accusing the British of sending Sullivan "to seduce us into a renunciation for our independence." Congress agreed to a conference, which accomplished nothing.

General Sullivan was finally released during a prisoner exchange and returned to Washington's army before the Battle of Trenton. It is important to note that General Sullivan's division secured the bridge over the Assunpink Creek to the north of the town. This stopped any escape, and thus many of the Hessian prisoners were captured. This route is now the main road entering Ewing Township, New Jersey, and is properly named "Sullivan's Way." In January 1777, General Sullivan took part in the Battle of Princeton.

Early in the year 1778, he was transferred to Rhode Island, where he led Continental troops and militia. His purpose was to work with the French naval fleet to besiege the British-held Newport, which was considered an important port and extremely vulnerable since France's entry into the Revolutionary efforts. Because of the damage of some of the French ships, and discouraged by the arrival of the British fleet, Charles Hector d'Estaing withdrew to Boston. The Sullivan garrison at Newport was then sortied, forcing General Sullivan into retreat after fighting in the Battle of Rhode Island in August 1778.

During the summer of 1779, General Sullivan led his expedition campaign against the Iroquois Indians in western New York. During the campaign, troops destroyed the Cayuga settlement called Coreorgonel, which is now the south side of Ithaca, New York. He forced his troops so hard that their horses became unusable, and they were forced to kill them on this campaign.

The general was tired and again opposed by Congress, so he retired from the army in 1779 and returned to New Hampshire. The British took advantage of this situation. British agents approached him and tried to persuade him to join them, to switch sides. The strategy failed.

In New Hampshire, he was considered a hero, and he returned as a delegate to the Continental Congress in 1780. In 1781, he was accused by Congress of being a foreign agent. He resigned from Congress on August 1781.

In 1782, New Hampshire named him the state's attorney general, and he served in that post until 1786. During those years, he was elected to the state assembly and served as the Speaker of the House. As a true Patriot, he led the drive to the ratification of the United States Constitution on June 21, 1788. He was elected president of the state (now governor) in 1786, 1787 and 1789.

After the new federal government was established, President Washington nominated him on September 24, 1789, to become the first federal judge for the United States District Court for the District of New Hampshire. He was confirmed and received his commission by the United States Senate on September 26, 1789.

Rogers' Rangers, 1755–1763

Rogers' Rangers was an independent militia that was attached to the British army during the French and Indian War. They were trained by Major Robert Rogers and were deployed as a light infantry force.

The rangers were never respected by the British regulars. However, Rogers' Rangers were one of the few non-Indian forces to operate in the Lake George and Lake Champlain region. After the British forces surrendered Fort William Henry in August 1757, the rangers were stationed on Rogers Island near Fort Edwards.

On July 7–8, 1758, Rogers' Rangers participated in the Battle of Carillon. In 1759, the rangers participated in one of the most celebrated operations, the St. Francis Raid. According to the records of Francis Parkman:

> They were ordered to destroy the Abenaki settlements of Saint-Francis in Quebec. It had been the base for raids and attacks of British settlements. Rogers led a force of 200 rangers from Crown Point deep into French territory. Following the October 3, 1759 attack and successful destruction of Saint-Francis, Rogers' force ran out of food during their retreat through the wilderness of northern New England. Once the Rangers reached a safe location along the Connecticut River at the abandoned Fort Wentworth, Rogers left them encamped. He returned a few days later with food and relief forces from Fort at Number 4 (Charlestown, New Hampshire), the nearest British outpost.
>
> In the raid on Saint-Francis, Rogers claimed 200 enemies were killed, leaving 20 women and children to be taken prisoners, of whom he took five children prisoners and let the rest go. The French recorded 30 deaths, including 20 women and children. Ranger casualties in the attack were one killed and six wounded; in the retreat, five were captured from one band of Rangers, and about 204 Rangers, allies and observers, about 100 returned.

At the beginning of the Revolutionary War, some rangers were among the minutemen at Lexington and Concord. Rogers himself offered to his help to

Robert Rogers, commander of Rogers' Rangers. *From Hobart Pillsbury's* New Hampshire: A History.

the commander of the colonial army. General Washington refused, thinking that Rogers was possibly a spy because he had just returned from England. It is interesting to note that Rogers later joined the British and formed the Queen's Rangers in 1776, as well as the King's Rangers later.

William Whipple Jr., 1730

William Whipple Jr., like many of the signers of the Declaration of Independence, was very supportive of the Revolutionary War. He served in the Continental Congress until 1779. In 1777, he was promoted to the rank of brigadier general of the New Hampshire militia. During his enlistment, he served in the Battles of Stillwater and Saratoga. In 1778, he raised another brigade of New Hampshire militia to fight in the Battle of Rhode Island.

General Whipple assisted in the capture of Burgoyne's army in Saratoga. He was one of the officers who arranged the surrender.

William maintained correspondence with family and friends while in Congress. These letters of correspondence provide a historic picture of the time. One excerpt follows:

General William Whipple, signer of the Declaration of Independence. *From Hobart Pillsbury's* New Hampshire: A History.

> *We are daily in expectation of some grand military operations in New York. The militia are all marching from this colony. The associators are mostly gone from this city, Colonels Kickinson, Cadwellader, etc., at the head of the regiment. No doubt in a very few days twenty thousand men, if not more, will be embodied in New Jersey, besides the army at York.*
>
> *This declaration has had a glorious effect, has made these colonies all alive, all the colonies forming governments, as you will see by the papers.*

After the war, Whipple became associate judge for the Supreme Court of New Hampshire. He died on November 28, 1785.

Weapons

The most popular infantry weapon used during the Revolution was the flintlock musket. This seventy-five-caliber musket was made for the British military. It was a smoothbore called the "Brown Bess." Other muskets used were the Charleville and the Kentucky long rifle. The muzzle-loaded musket was used by both the British and American Continental troops. These weapons were most commonly equipped with bayonets for close-order combat. They were only accurate in a range between fifty to one hundred yards. Some American light troops carried rifles, which were considered more accurate and had a longer range, but they took longer to reload. The officers in the Continental army were known to carry sidearms (flintlock pistols), but they were not as accurate beyond a very short range. The pistol was popular for use in duels and was more of a personal weapon.

The sword and sabre were used mostly by officers and were highly ornamented. Generals like George Washington wore their swords as part of their dress uniforms.

Both the British and Americans made use of artillery weapons. These cannons could fire a variety of projectiles. The most popular cannon used in the war was the mobile three-pounder, known as a "galloper gun," which could fire a three-pound projectile and the heavier six-pound projectile. Like many of the weapons, the artillery pieces were often captured by the American army from the British. A good example of this took place when the Continental army captured Boston in March 1776 and used British artillery pieces that had been seized by General Knox from the British fort at Ticonderoga.

Chapter 6

THE MAJOR FORTS IN THE WAR

FORT CONSTITUTION

According to the Fort Constitution Historic Site, operated by State of New Hampshire State Parks:

> *In 1791 the state of New Hampshire gave the country the neck of land on which Fort William and Mary and a lighthouse were situated. The fort was repaired, renamed Fort Constitution and garrisoned with a company of United States artillery. Renovations which included a wall twice as high as that of the colonial fort and new brick buildings were completed in 1808. It is the ruins of this old fort that are seen today. The fort was used during the War of 1812 and was still serviceable during the Civil War when various units were trained there.*
>
> *Improvements in artillery during the nineteenth century made it clear the old fort would have to be replaced. A new one was begun during the Civil War. It was to be a massive, three-tiered granite structure, but like others begun at the same time, was never completed. Armored steam powered warships with heavy guns made the masonry fort obsolete.*
>
> *Outside the old fort in the area now occupied by the Coast Guard, a completely new system of fortifications were built between 1897 and 1903. This included a battery of two eight inch guns on disappearing carriages, a mines casement, cable tank and a storage house for mines. The harbor was protected by mines during the Spanish American War and during World War I and II. Fort Constitution was returned to the state in 1961 and placed on the National Register of Historic Places on July 2, 1973.*

Fort McClary, 1720–1918

Fort McClary was considered a sentinel on the Piscataqua, which was itself an important military defense of Portsmouth in 1689. This tract of land was owned by William Pepperrell, a wealthy merchant and landowner who also owned at tract of land known as the Battery Pasture. The first building was possibly a small blockhouse or a simple earthwork. This fortification was known at Pepperrell's garrison, or Fort Pepperrell.

When the war broke out in 1775, the Pepperrell family remained loyal to the British Crown. However, the local townspeople confiscated all the property belonging to the family, including the fort. The fort was manned by the New Hampshire militia until 1779 and later abandoned.

In 1808, the federal government ceded the 1.89 acres of land to the State of Massachusetts in order to build a new "Second System" fort. The new fort was renamed Fort McClary in honor of New Hampshire native Major Andrew McClary

In 1844, a large blockhouse (which still exists today) was built, replacing the upper battery. In 1846, twenty-five additional acres were purchased by the federal government, bringing its total land area close to its present size.

After 1846, the fort was deactivated, it wasn't until the Civil War began in 1861 that the fort was brought back to life. Much of the fort was in disrepair during this period, and all the hardware and guns were scrapped or sold by 1910. The fort was not garrisoned during this time, except for a brief period in 1898 that saw a detachment from Fort Constitution in New Castle.

During the First World War, the blockhouse was used as a lookout post, which aided Fort Constitution and Fort Foster for the defense of the Portsmouth harbor.

In 1918, the fort again was deactivated. In 1924, the federal government transferred most of its property of 25.58 acres to the State of Maine, except for the original 1.87 acres containing the old buildings. Without proper maintenance, the building had fallen into ruins. It is recorded that the second riflemen's house was razed in 1928 for safety reasons. According to photographs of the fort, the barracks still existed at that time. The Town of Kittery managed the park for several years until 1937 before the State of Maine took over the responsibility of preserving the property.

From 1942 to 1945, the blockhouse was again used as a lookout post by civil defense units for spotting aircraft and ships in the harbor.

In 1969, Fort McClary was placed on the National Register of Historic Places. The blockhouse was refurbished in 1987. This fine old fort is open to the public. The fort was not garrisoned at all after 1905.

FORT AT NUMBER 4

The Fort at Number 4 was located at the northernmost British settlement along the Connecticut River in New Hampshire until after the French and Indian War. The location is presently known as Charlestown. Construction of a log fort began in 1740 by brothers Stephen, Samuel and David Farnsworth. By 1743, there were about ten families settled in a square of interconnected houses, enclosed in a stockade with a guard tower.

The fort is said to have been 180 feet long with log flankers at the corners to give a raking fire along each side of the fort, thus discouraging firing or scaling parties. Within the enclosure were six log houses placed against the walls. As Charlestown was for many years the most advanced northern white settlement, it was continually attacked by the French and Indian forces. A fort here was considered strategically important to the area.

The fort, under the command of Captain Phineas Stevens, was besieged in 1747 by four hundred French and Indians who eventually withdrew to Canada. This battle, the last in the fifteen-years conflict with the French, marked the beginning of English supremacy in northern New England.

During the end of the French and Indian War, many soldiers were stationed in the fort in order to protect Charlestown and the frontier of the north country of New Hampshire, and it was a military base from which colonial troops passed to assist Lord Amherst in his struggle to obtain Crown Point, New York. Number 4 was also a rendezvous for General Stark and his New Hampshire troops en route to the Battle of Bennington. Other regiments that were stationed there included Colonel Nathan Whiting's regiment of Connecticut and Colonel John Goffe's New Hampshire Provincial Regiment.

According to New Hampshire historians and the Visitor Information Service:

> *General Jeffrey Amherst ordered a road to be built between the fort and another fort which was newly captured at Crown Point, located on the shore of Lake Champlain in New York. Consequently, Captain John Stark and a company of Rangers, together with Colonel Goffe's Regiment, built the Crown Point Military Road. It was 77.5 miles long, with many*

blockhouses along its route to protect supplies and travelers through the wilderness that would later become Vermont. With the defeat of the French in 1761, and the Treaty of Paris in 1763, the need for the fort ended.

The Fort at Number 4 is presently used as a living museum, which was recreated to depict its appearance during the King George's War. It is well known in New Hampshire historical societies that during the summer, the fort hosts both French and Indian War and American Revolutionary War reenactments. Members of the public are cordially invited to visit the Fort at Number 4.

Fort Stark

New Hampshire State Parks noted that "Fort Stark State Historic Site is located on a peninsula historically called Jerry's Point on the southeast corner of New Castle Island. Fort Stark was name in honor of John Stark, commander of New Hampshire forces at the Battle of Bennington (1777)."

As Portsmouth Harbor's importance increased with its Revolutionary War shipbuilding industry and the establishment if the Portsmouth Naval Shipyards in 1800, additional fortification was needed.

The final coastal fortification occurred during World War II. The five remaining fort are obsolete and considered as historic sites or parks, which are open to the public. After World War II, the navy took over the installation and used Fort Stark primarily for reserve training until it was deeded to the State of New Hampshire in 1978.

Fort Sullivan

According to the archives of Fort Sullivan's history, the site of Fort Sullivan was originally used in 1775 when the New Hampshire militia, commanded by General John Sullivan, built an earthwork defense on the bluff so as to guard the channel to Portsmouth. The fort later used for the British-American War of 1812. In 1863, the fort was rebuilt to defend Portsmouth Harbor during the Civil War and any attacks from the Confederate navy. After 1866, the fort was dismantled. Nearby the site was erected Camp Long, named for Secretary of the Navy John Long during the Spanish-American War. During a short period of time in 1898, the stockade housed 1,612 Spanish prisoners, until they were returned to Spain.

When Camp Long was dismantled in 1901, the site was made available for a naval prison. The construction took place between the years 1905 and 1908 and was modeled after Alcatraz. Besides the navy, marine inmates were also housed here. During World War I, the prison housed a maximum of 2,295 inmates in 1918. In 1942, a northeast wing was added, and in 1943, a southwest wing doubled the fortress, which rises beside the rocky shore at Portsmouth Harbor. The maximum occupancy reached 3,088 in 1945.

In 2001, historian Richard Fabrizio provided the "dead in the water" naval prison plans:

> *The building was previously one of 14 structures the Portsmouth Naval Shipyard had considered for out leasing and renovation. Local developer Joseph Sawtelle estimated the cost to renovate the immense edifice into civilian office space, including removing lead paint and asbestos, would cost more than $10 million. But plans to adapt the prison were halted a month after Sawtelle's death in 2000, and abandoned altogether after military base security was tightened following the terrorist attacks of September 11, 2001 in New York City, and Washington D.C.*

FORT WASHINGTON

Fort Washington was built in 1775 on Peirce Island by order of Major General John Sullivan, who was the commander of Portsmouth Harbor, to protect the Piscataqua River at the channel and to provide crossfire with Fort Sullivan. There was also constructed a log boom defense placed in the river between the two forts.

The fort was garrisoned by 180 troops, commanded by Captain Titus Salter from 1775 to 1778. Later, Peirce Island was renamed Isle of Washington during the American Revolution in honor of General George Washington. During the War of 1812, the fort was repaired and regarrisoned when British warships blockaded the coast of the United States. The fort was probably not used at all during the Civil War.

The fort last saw military service in 1941 when Peirce Island became the location of an Army Recreation Center—a tent camp for more than five hundred troops.

The outer breastworks of the fort still remain but are completely overgrown. There are, however, historic markers of the fort and the Portsmouth Naval Shipyard across the Piscataqua River, as well as some panels on the history of the island and river. The park is open to the public.

Fort Wentworth

Fort Wentworth was constructed by order of Benning Wentworth in 1755. The fort was established at the junction of the Upper Ammonoosuc River and the Connecticut River in Northumberland by the soldiers of Colonel Joseph Blanchard's New Hampshire Provincial Regiment, including Robert Rogers.

During the American Revolutionary War, Jeremiah Eames's company of rangers garrisoned and repaired the unused fort from 1776 to 1778 in order to protect northern New Hampshire from attack from the British in nearby Canada. Until the end of the war in 1783, other New Hampshire militia used part of the garrison.

Timothy Walker House and Fort

The Timothy Walker House and Fort (a garrison at Rumford, now Concord, New Hampshire) was one of several strong points and massacre sites. Despite these precautionary measures, an attack from Native Americans took place at this fort on August 11, 1746. Five men were killed, and two were carried off as captives.

Reverend Timothy Walker was said to have been the best shot in Concord. He never went to church without his rifle. Most of the men in each family were armed in church with their rifle cocked and ready for an attack.

Garrison of Reverend Timothy Walker. *Author's collection.*

FORT WILLIAM AND MARY

The fort is located on a peninsula on the northeast corner of New Castle Island. The present fort, named Fort Constitution, is one of seven forts built to protect Portsmouth Harbor.

The first installation of this site was an earthwork fort with four "great guns" erected in 1632. Later, it was followed by a wooden blockhouse, which was built in 1666. By the time, William and Mary were on the thrown of England, a strong rivalry with France had developed and stronger defenses were required. Cannons and military stores were sent from England in 1692, and a breastwork was constructed to protect them. Each breastwork was a rampart of turf three feet high on which batteries of guns were clamped on wooden platforms protected by a stone wall about seven feet high.

The following Revolutionary War event has been recorded by New Hampshire State Parks:

> *It was on the eve of the Revolution the fort played its most dramatic role in history. On December 13, 1774, Paul Revere rode from Boston with a*

message that the fort at Rhode Island had been dismantled and troops were coming to take over Fort William and Mary. The following day the drums beat to collect the Sons of Liberty, and 400 men from Portsmouth, Rye and New Castle raided the fort and removed 98 barrels of gun powder.

The next night a small party led by John Sullivan carried off sixteen pieces of small cannon and military stores. This raid took place months before the incidents at Concord and Lexington, and was an important event in the chain of events leading to the revolution. Governor John Wentworth immediately sent to Boston for help. The sloop Canceaux arrived December 17, followed two days later the frigate Scarborough. The latter had forty guns and carried one hundred British marines on board. This prevented further raids by the patriots, but produced a dangerous state of tension.

By the summer of 1775 Governor Wentworth and his family took refuge in the fort and lived there two months in hope that a conflict should be avoided. Finally on August 24, 1775, the governor and his family sailed to Boston on the Scarborough. Wentworth made a brief visit a month later when, from the Isles of Shoals, he issued a proclamation discontinuing the assembly. This was the last act of royal authority in New Hampshire.

SUMMARY OF NEW HAMPSHIRE FORTS

The following lists of New Hampshire forts were compiled by Pete Payette.

Eastern New Hampshire Forts

Fort Anglesea, Brentwood Garrisons, Castle Fort, Clark's Points Redoubt, Camp Constitution, Fort Constitution, Battery Cumberland, Damme Garrison, Fort Dearborn, Dearborn Garrison, Dover Garrison, Dover Meetinghouse, Durham Garrison, Epping Garrison, Exeter Garrisons, Exeter Powder House, Camp Fry, Gilman Garrison, Great Fort, Green Garrison, Greenland Garrisons, Hampton Garrisons, Hampton Falls Garrison, Hampton Meetinghouse, Fort Hancock, Hilton's Point, fort at Jaffrey's Point, battery at Jerry's Point, Kingston Garrison, Camp Langdon, Lee Garrison, Madbury Garrison, Camp Morley, Newfields Garrison, Newington Garrison, Newmarket Garrison, New Res, Oyster River, Pannaway, Pascataway, Portsmouth Arsenal, Portsmouth Garrisons, Portsmouth Gun House, Portsmouth Powder House, Rollinsford

Garrisons, Rye Garrisons, Seabrook Garrison, Shaw's Hill Fort, South Mill Pond Barracks, Fort Star, Fort Stark, Stratham Garrison, Strawbery Banke, Castle Walbach, Walbach Tower, Fort Washington and Fort (Castle) William and Mary.

Western and Central New Hampshire Forts

Abenaki Fort, Alstead Forts, Amherst Garrisons, Fort Atkinson, Barrington Garrison, Bedford Garrisons, Camp Belknap, Bellows's Garrison, Camp Berry, Butler's Garrison, Call Garrison, Canterbury Garrison, Chester Garrison, Concord Garrisons, Fort Contoocook, Cromwell's Trade Post, Derry Garrisons, Fort Eddy, Epsom Blockhouse, Flagg's Garrison, Gault's Garrison, Gilmanton Garrisons, Great Meadows Fort, Fort Hinsdale, Hinsdale Garrisons, Hinsdale Indian Fort, Hopkinton Garrisons, How's Fort, Hudson Garrisons, Irish Fort, Johnston's Garrison, Fort Keene, Camp Keyes, Longfellow Garrison, Lovewell's Fort, Lyndeborough Garrison, Manchester Garrisons, Milford Garrisons, Morse's Garrison, Nashua Garrisons, Newichawannock Blockhouse, North Haverhill Garrison, Northumberland Fort, Nottingham Blockhouse, Fort at Number 4, Fort at Number 2, Pembroke Garrisons, Penacook Fort, Penacook Indian Fort, Peterborough Fort, Camp Ramsdell, Rochester Garrisons, Camp Rockingham, Salem Garrisons, Salisbury Fort, Fort Shattuck, Squamanagonic Blockhouse, Stark's Fort, Fort Stephens, Stratfort Ford, Suncook Fort, Swanzey Garrisons, Waldron's Trade Post, Walpole Fort, Weirs Blockhouse, Fort Wentworth, Willard's Trade Post, Winchester Garrisons and Fort Winnipesaukee.

Appendix

The Declaration of Independence of the United States of America

In Congress, July 4, 1776

The unanimous Declaration of the thirteen united States of America,

When in the Course of human events, it becomes necessary for one people to dissolve the political bands which have connected them with another, and to assume among the powers of the earth, the separate and equal station to which the Laws of Nature and of Nature's God entitle them, a decent respect to the opinions of mankind requires that they should declare the causes which impel them to the separation.

We hold these truths to be self-evident, that all men are created equal, that they are endowed by their Creator with certain unalienable Rights, that among these are Life, Liberty and the pursuit of Happiness.

That to secure these rights, Governments are instituted among Men, deriving their just powers from the consent of the governed, That whenever any Form of Government becomes destructive of these ends, it is the Right of the People to alter or to abolish it, and to institute new Government, laying its foundation on such principles and organizing its powers in such form, as to them shall seem most likely to effect their Safety and Happiness. Prudence, indeed, will dictate that Governments long established should not be changed for light and transient causes; and accordingly all experience hath shewn, that mankind are more disposed to suffer, while evils are sufferable, than to right themselves by abolishing the forms to which they are accustomed. But when a long train of abuses and usurpations, pursuing invariably the same Object evinces a design to reduce them under absolute Despotism, it is their right, it is their duty, to throw off such Government, and to provide new Guards for their future security.

Such has been the patient sufferance of these Colonies; and such is now the necessity which constrains them to alter their former Systems of Government. The history of the present King of Great Britain is a history of repeated injuries and usurpations, all having in direct object the establishment of an absolute Tyranny over these States. To prove this, let Facts be submitted to a candid world. He has refused his Assent to Laws, the most wholesome and necessary for the public good. He has forbidden his Governors to pass Laws of immediate and pressing importance, unless suspended in their operation till his Assent should be obtained; and when so suspended, he has utterly neglected to attend to them. He has refused to pass other Laws for the accommodation of large districts of people, unless those people would relinquish the right of Representation in the Legislature, a right inestimable to them and formidable to tyrants only. He has called together legislative bodies at places unusual, uncomfortable, and distant from the depository of their Public Records, for the sole purpose of fatiguing them into compliance with his measures. He has dissolved Representative Houses repeatedly, for opposing with manly firmness of his invasions on the rights of the people. He has refused for a long time, after such dissolutions, to cause others to be elected, whereby the Legislative Powers, incapable of Annihilation, have returned to the People at large for their exercise; the State remaining in the mean time exposed to all the dangers of invasion from without, and convulsions within. He has endeavoured to prevent the population of these States; for that purpose obstructing the Laws for Naturalization of Foreigners; refusing to pass others to encourage their migrations hither, and raising the conditions of new Appropriations of Lands. He has obstructed the Administration of Justice by refusing his Assent to Laws for establishing Judiciary Powers. He has made Judges dependent on his Will alone for the tenure of their offices, and the amount and payment of their salaries. He has erected a multitude of New Offices, and sent hither swarms of Officers to harass our people and eat out their substance. He has kept among us, in times of peace, Standing Armies without the Consent of our legislatures. He has affected to render the Military independent of and superior to the Civil Power. He has combined with others to subject us to a jurisdiction foreign to our constitution, and unacknowledged by our laws; giving his Assent to their Acts of pretended Legislation: For quartering large bodies of armed troops among us: For protecting them, by a mock Trial from punishment for any Murders which they should commit on the Inhabitants of these States: For cutting off our Trade with all parts of the world: For imposing Taxes on us without our Consent: For depriving us in many cases, of the benefit of Trial by Jury: For transporting us beyond Seas to be tried for pretended offences: For abolishing the free System of English Laws in a neighbouring Province, establishing therein an Arbitrary government, and enlarging its Boundaries so as to render it at once an example and fit instrument for introducing the same absolute rule into these Colonies: For taking away our Charters, abolishing our most valuable Laws and altering fundamentally the Forms of our Governments: For suspending our own Legislatures, and declaring themselves invested with power to legislate for us in all cases whatsoever. He has abdicated Government here, by declaring us out of his Protection and waging War against us. He has plundered our seas, ravaged our coasts, burnt our towns, and destroyed the lives of our people. He is at this time transporting large Armies of foreign Mercenaries to compleat the works of death, desolation, and tyranny, already begun with circumstances of Cruelty & Perfidy scarcely paralleled in the most barbarous ages, and totally unworthy the Head of a civilized nation. He has constrained our fellow Citizens taken Captive on the high Seas to bear Arms against their Country, to become the executioners of their friends and Brethren, or to fall themselves by their Hands. He has excited domestic insurrections amongst us, and has endeavoured to bring on the inhabitants of our frontiers, the merciless Indian Savages whose known rule of warfare, is an undistinguished destruction of all ages, sexes and conditions. In every stage of these Oppressions We have Petitioned for Redress in the most humble terms: Our repeated Petitions have been answered only by repeated injury. A Prince, whose character is thus marked by every act which may define a Tyrant, is unfit to be the ruler of a free people.

Nor have We been wanting in attentions to our British brethren. We have warned them from time to time of attempts by their legislature to extend an unwarrantable jurisdiction over us. We have reminded them of the circumstances of our emigration and settlement here. We have appealed to their native justice and magnanimity, and we have conjured them by the ties of our common kindred to disavow these usurpations, which, would inevitably interrupt our connections and correspondence. They too have been deaf to the voice of justice and of consanguinity. We must, therefore, acquiesce in the necessity, which denounces our Separation, and hold them, as we hold the rest of mankind, Enemies in War, in Peace Friends.

We, therefore, the Representatives of the united States of America, in General Congress, Assembled, appealing to the Supreme Judge of the world for the rectitude of our intentions, do, in the Name, and by Authority of the good People of these Colonies, solemnly publish and declare, That these united Colonies are, and of Right ought to be Free and Independent States; that they are Absolved from all Allegiance to the British Crown, and that all political connection between them and the State of Great Britain, is and ought to be totally dissolved; and that as Free and Independent States, they have full Power to levy War, conclude Peace, contract Alliances, establish Commerce, and to do all other Acts and Things which Independent States may of right do. And for the support of this Declaration, with a firm reliance on the protection of divine Providence, we mutually pledge to each other our Lives, our Fortunes and our sacred Honor.

Signed in Congress by the Representatives of the Thirteen United States of America.

BIBLIOGRAPHY

Alexander Scammell to George Washington, November 16, 1780. Letter. Library of Congress.

American Revolutionary War: Guilford Courthouse. Washington, D.C.: Department of the Interior, National Park Service, n.d.

Anderson, Fred. *Crucible of War: Seven Years' War and the Fate of Empire in British North America, 1754–1766.* New York: Alfred A. Knopf, 2000.

———. *The War that Made America.* New York: Viking, 2005.

Bacon, Edwin M. *Boston: A Guide Book.* Boston: Ginn & Company, 1922.

Baker, Henry M. *New Hampshire in the Battle of Bunker Hill.* Boston, 1903.

Bancroft, George. *History of the United States, from the Discovery of the American Continent.* Vol. 4. Boston: Little, Brown and Company, 1856.

Bell, Charles Henry. *Exeter in 1776.* Exeter, NH: News-letter Press, 1876.

Bellows's Regiment of Militia. Manchester, NH: State Buildings Publishing, 1903.

Bisbee, Ernest E. *The White Mountain Scrap Book.* Lancaster, NH: Bisnee Press, 1946.

Blythe, Bob. *John Paul Jones (1747–1792).* Washington, D.C.: Department of the Interior, National Park Service, n.d.

Boatner, Mark M., III. *Encyclopedia of the American Revolution.* Mechanicsburg, PA: Stackpole Books, 1994.

Bourgoing-Alarie, Marie-Eve. "Mieux vant que jamais." *L'Hebdo Journal* (2009).

Carver, Robin. *History of Boston.* Boston: Lilly, Wait, Colman and Holden, 1834.

Chartrand, Rene. *Ticonderoga 1758: Montcalm's Against All Odds.* Oxford, England: Osprey Publishing, 2000.

Collins, Varnum Lansing. *A Brief Narrative of the Ravages of the British and Hessians at Princeton in 1776–1777.* New York: New York Times and Armo Press, 1968.

Crockett, Walter H. *Vermont: The Green Mountain State.* Vol. 2. New York: Century History Company, 1921.

Ferling, John. *Almost a Miracle: The American Victory in the War of Independence.* Oxford, England: Oxford University Press, 2009.

Fisher, David H. *Washington's Crossing.* New York: Oxford University Press, 2004.

Furneaux, Rupert. *The Battle of Saratoga.* New York: Stein and Day, 1971.

Gibson, Lawrence Henry. *The British Empire Before the American Revolution.* Vol. 7. New York: Knopf. 1965.

Gilman, Nicholas. *Biographical Directory of the United States Congress.* N.p., n.d.

Gruber, Ira. *The Howe Brothers and the American Revolution.* New York: Atheneum Press, 1972.

A Guide to the Granite State. American Guide Series, New Hampshire. Boston: Houghton Mifflin Company, 1938.

Guthorn, Peter J. *American Maps and Map Makers of the Revolution.* Monmouth Beach, NJ: Philip Freneau Press, 1966.

Harris, John. *Lexington—Concord.* Boston: Globe Newspaper Company, 1975.

———. *Washington's First Visit: The Liberation of Boston.* Boston: Globe Newspaper Company, 1976.

Howe, M.A. DeWolfe. *Boston: The Place and the People.* New York: Macmillan & Company, 1903.

Illustrated Historical and Biographical Record of the State of New Hampshire. Manchester, NH: State Building Publishing, 1903.

Johnston, Henry P. *The Storming of Stony Point on the Hudson.* New York: James T. White & Company, 1900.

Ketchum, Richard M. *Saratoga: Turning Point of America's Revolutionary War.* New York: Henry Holt, 1997.

McLennan, J.S. *Louisbourg: From Its Founding to Its Fall.* London: Macmillan and Company, 1918.

Millard, James P. "The Battle of Lake George, Sept. 8, 1755." Lake Champlain and Lake George Historic Site, America's Historic Lakes. http://www.historiclakes.org/wm_henry/lg_battle.html.

Morrissey, Hoffman. *Saratoga 1777: Turning Point of a Revolution.* Oxford, England: Osprey Publishing, 2000.

Nester, William R. *The First Global War: Britain, France, and the Fate of North America, 1756–1775.* Westport, CT: Praeger, 2000.

Nickerson, Hoffman. *The Turning Point of a Revolution.* Port Washington, NY: Kennikat, 1967. First published in 1928.

Palmer, Peter S. *History of Lake Champlain, from Its First Exploration by the French in 1609 to the Close of the Year 1814.* New York: Frank F. Lovell and Company, 1886.

Parkman, Francis. *Montcalm and Wolfe.* Vol. 1. Boston: Little, Brown and Company, 1922.

Pillsbury, Hobart. *New Hampshire: A History.* New York: Lewis Historical Publishing Company, 1927.

Potter, C.E. *The History of Manchester, formerly Derryfield, in New Hampshire, Including that of Ancient Amoskeag, or the Middle Merrimack Valley.* Manchester, NH: C.E. Potter, Publisher, 1856.

————. *The Military History of the State of New Hampshire, from Its Settlement in 1623 to the Rebellion in 1861.* Concord, NH: Rumford Press, 1866.

Randall, Peter E. *New Hampshire Years of Revolution.* Concord, NH: Profile Publications & the New Hampshire Bicentennial Commission, 1976.

Reid, Stuart. *Quebec, 1759: The Battle that Won Canada.* Oxford, England: Osprey Publishing, n.d.

Reid, W. Max. *The Story of Old Fort Johnson.* New York: G.P. Putnan's Sons, 1906.

Rosal, Lorenca Consuelo. *God Save the People: A New Hampshire History.* Oxford, NH: Equity, 1988.

Roy-Sole, Monique. *Trois-Rivieres: A Tale of Tenacity.* N.p.: Canadian Geographic, 2009.

Stanhope, Philip Henry. *History of England.* London, United Kingdom, 1854.

Starbuck, David. *Massacre at Fort William Henry.* Hanover, NH: University Press of New England, 2002.

Steele, Ian K. *Betrayals: Fort William Henry & the Massacre.* New York: Oxford University Press, 1990.

Trevelyan, Sir George Otto. *The American Revolution, 1766–1776.* London: Longmans, Green, 1903.

Trustee of the Boston Public Library. *Blood in the Streets: The Boston Massacre.* Boston: Revolutionary War Bicentennial Commission, 1970.

Whipple, William, Jr. *Brigadier General of the New Hampshire Militia.* Manchester, NH: Historical & Biographical Records for the State of New Hampshire, 1903. Also found in the New Hampshire State Archives, Concord, New Hampshire.

INDEX

A

Abenakis 11
Adams, John 21, 26, 69, 102
Ammonoosuc River 112
Assunpink Creek 59, 102

B

Bartlett, Josiah 27, 51, 67, 83
Battle of Bemis Heights 63, 93
Battle of Bennington 60, 76, 77, 78, 85, 97, 109, 110
Battle of Bunker Hill 28, 36, 37, 46, 94, 97
Battle of Carillon 15, 16, 103
Battle of Fort St. Jean 75
Battle of Freeman's Farm 63, 76, 77, 93, 96
Battle of King's Bridge 96
Battle of Lake George 10, 86
Battle of Lexington 34
Battle of Long Island 100
Battle of Monmouth (Battle of Monmouth Courthouse) 64, 85, 93
Battle of Newton 93

Battle of Princeton 59, 96, 98, 102
Battle of Rhode Island 84, 102, 105
Battle of Stillwater 84, 105
Battle of Stony Point 66
Battle of The Cedars 75
Battle of the Plains of Abraham (Battle of Quebec) 9, 16
Battle of Trenton 56, 57, 58, 96, 98, 102
Battle of Trois-Rivieres 54
Battle of Yorktown 85
Battles of Lexington and Concord 73, 92, 94, 97, 103
Battles of Saratoga 62, 63, 78, 84, 92, 93, 105
Bedel, Colonel Timothy 47, 54, 74, 84, 85
Bemis Heights 63, 64, 93, 96
Bennington, Vermont 60, 62, 99
Blanchard, Joseph 7, 11, 112
Bonhomme Richard 80, 88
Boston, Massachusetts 21, 23, 28, 32, 35, 36, 37, 38, 40, 48, 62, 88, 94, 97, 98, 100, 102, 106

Breed's Hill 38, 40, 41, 97
Broeck, Abraham 64
Bunker Hill 28, 36, 37, 38, 39, 42, 43, 45, 46, 94, 97
Burgoyne, General John 56, 60, 62, 63, 64, 75, 76, 77, 84, 87, 92, 105

C

Cambridge, Massachusetts 28, 38, 40, 41, 43, 97
Charlestown, New Hampshire 8, 32, 38, 50, 76, 77, 103, 109
Clinton, General Henry 64, 65, 66
Cochran, John 28
Committee of Safety 36, 37, 38, 39, 50, 67, 83, 84
Concord, New Hampshire 30, 51, 112
Confiscation Act 82
Connecticut River 47, 54, 109, 112
Continental army 56, 58, 59, 63, 64, 66, 68, 73, 74, 75, 76, 78, 85, 86, 87, 88, 92, 94, 98, 99, 106

Copp's Hill 40
Cornwallis, General
 Charles 59, 60, 65,
 67, 69, 85
Crown Point 7, 9, 10, 84,
 86, 100, 109

D

Dartmouth College 62
Dawes, William 30
Dearborn, Captain Henry
 48, 85
Declaration of Independence
 46, 51, 53, 105
Delaware, Maryland 57
Delaware River 56, 57,
 58, 88, 96
Durham, New Hampshire
 28, 86

E

Erdman, Jean, Baron de
 Dieskau 10, 11,
 12, 86
Exeter, New Hampshire
 26, 28, 34, 46, 50,
 62, 76, 86, 88, 92

F

Fitzgerald, Colonel John 57
Folsom, Colonel Nathaniel
 11, 34, 46, 86
Fort Carillon (Fort
 Ticonderoga) 10,
 15, 16, 54, 56, 57,
 62, 64, 76, 78, 87,
 92, 93, 96, 97, 98
Fort Constitution 107,
 108, 113
Fort Edwards 8, 10, 11,
 12, 14, 91, 103
Fort McClary 108, 109
Fortress Louisbourg 9,
 84, 91

Fort Stark 110
Fort St. Frederic 10, 12
Fort Sullivan 47, 110, 111
Fort Washington 46, 111
Fort Wentworth 103, 112
Fort William and Mary
 28, 71, 86, 100,
 113, 114
Fort William Henry 8, 12,
 13, 103
Frederick, George William
 (King George III)
 6, 19, 21
Freeman's Farm 63, 76,
 77, 85, 93, 96
French and Indian War 6, 8,
 9, 13, 84, 86, 91, 92,
 93, 97, 103, 109, 110

G

Gates, General Horatio
 56, 63, 75, 76, 85,
 87, 93
Germantown, Pennsylvania
 94
Gilman, Captain Nicholas
 62, 86, 87, 88
Gilman, Colonel David 56
Gilman, Colonel Peter 7
Greene, General Nathanael
 56, 58, 65
Green Mountain Boys 60,
 77, 99

H

Halifax, Nova Scotia 8,
 15, 27, 91, 98
Harvard College 20, 38
Hay, John 69
Howe, General William 6,
 40, 56, 98, 100

I

Isaac Royall House 97

J

Jones, John Paul 35, 79,
 80, 88, 90

K

Keene, New Hampshire 9
Kentucky long rifle 106
Kilburn, John 9
Knox, General Henry 58,
 78, 106

L

Lafayette, Marquis de 65
Lake Champlain 15, 16,
 48, 76, 87, 103, 109
Lake George 10, 12, 86, 103
Lexington, Massachusetts
 30, 32, 34, 35, 73, 92,
 94, 97, 103
"Liberty Tree" 21, 22
Lincoln, General Benjamin
 63, 64, 93, 99
Londonderry, New
 Hampshire 62, 82,
 83, 94, 97
Lunenberg, Massachusetts 93

M

Manchester, New
 Hampshire 60, 99
Medford, Massachusetts
 35, 42, 45, 50, 97
Meserve, Colonel George 8
Meserve, Colonel Nathaniel
 7, 91
minutemen 35, 98, 103
Mississippi River 17, 69
Monmouth Courthouse 64, 65
Monro, Colonel George 12,
 13, 14
Montcalm, General Louis-
 Joseph de 8, 9, 12,
 14, 15, 16, 17

Montgomery, General Richard 48, 92
Moore, Colonel Daniel 62, 76
Motier, Major General Gilbert du 65

N

National Park Service 88, 89, 90
New Castle Island 28, 54, 76, 108, 110, 113
New Hampshire regiments
  Bedel's 74
  Bellows's 75
  Chase's 75
  Drake's 75
  Evans's 76
  First 7, 96
  Hobart's 76
  Long's 76
  Moore's 76
  Moulton's 77
  Nichols's 77
  Second 7, 35, 74, 78, 96
  Stickney's 77
  Third 35, 74, 77, 78, 87
Newmarket, New Hampshire 28
North Church (Christ Church) 39
Northumberland, New Hampshire 112

P

Percy, General Hugh 32, 33
Pickering, John 27
Pickering, Thomas 28
Piscataqua River 28, 46, 108, 111, 112
Plymouth, Massachusetts 20, 76, 95
Poor, Colonel Enoch 34, 67, 74, 92, 93
Portsmouth, New Hampshire 92

Prescott, Colonel Henry 27, 36, 38, 39, 43, 98
Preston, Captain Thomas 23, 25
Princeton, New Jersey 56, 59, 60, 96, 98, 102
Proscription Act 81, 82
Prospect Hill 88
Provincial Congress 34, 36, 37, 44, 48, 51, 84, 100

Q

Quebec, Canada 9, 15, 16, 48, 54, 64, 85, 100

R

Rall, Colonel Johann 58
Read, Colonel Seth 41, 43
Reed, Colonel James 93, 94, 97
Reed, Colonel Joseph 57
Revere, Paul 28, 30, 100, 113
Rhode Island 77, 84, 102, 105, 114
Rogers' Rangers 8, 9, 97, 103
Rogers, Robert 8, 9, 97, 103, 104, 112

S

Saratoga, New York 60, 62, 63, 64, 69, 78, 84, 85, 87, 92, 93, 94, 96, 105
Scammell, Alexander 67, 86, 87, 95, 96
Stamp Act 21, 22
Stark, Cabel 73
Stark, Colonel John 8, 34, 42, 43, 44, 60, 61, 62, 73, 76, 77, 85, 94, 96, 97, 98, 99, 109, 110
St. Francis 8, 9, 103
Stony Point 66, 67
Sullivan, General John 46, 48, 50, 54, 56, 58,

59, 77, 85, 93, 94, 100, 102, 110, 111

T

Thornton, Matthew 36, 46, 51, 83, 84
Timothy Walker House 112
Treaty of Aix-la-Chapelle 7, 92
Treaty of Paris 17, 69, 110
Trenton, New Jersey 56, 57, 58, 59, 94, 98, 102

W

Walker, Timothy 82
Ward, Colonel Samuel 38, 48
Washington, General George 6, 48, 54, 56, 57, 58, 59, 60, 64, 65, 66, 68, 69, 78, 85, 87, 88, 90, 92, 93, 94, 96, 98, 100, 102, 103, 104, 106, 111
Weare, Meshech 48
Wentworth, Governor Benning 92, 112
Wentworth, Governor John 26, 27, 29, 81, 83, 86, 92, 100, 114
West Point Military Academy, New York 67, 78, 90
Wheelock, Captain John 62
Whipple, William, Jr. 51, 75, 76, 84, 105
Whitcomb, Benjamin 78
Whitcomb's Rangers 78
White Plains, New York 94
Wingate, General Joshua 54
Wood Creek 11

Y

Yorktown 46, 68, 69, 73, 85, 88, 96

ABOUT THE AUTHOR

D r. Bruce D. Heald, PhD, is a graduate of Boston University, the University of Massachusetts–Lowell and Columbia Pacific University. He is an adjunct associate professor at Babes-Bolyai University, Cluj, Romania, and presently an adjunct professor of American History at Plymouth State University, Plymouth, New Hampshire. Dr. Heald is presently a fellow in the International Biographical Association and the World Literary Academy in Cambridge, England. He is the recipient of the Gold Medal of Honor for the literary achievement from the American Biographical Institute (1993). From 2005 to 2008, he was a state representative to the General Court of New Hampshire. He resides in Meredith, New Hampshire, with his family.

CPSIA information can be obtained
at www.ICGtesting.com
Printed in the USA
BVOW09*0814250218
509040BV00006B/36/P